Group Training Techniques

Editors: M L and P J BERGER

GW00691877

Gower

First published 1972 in Great Britain by
Gower Press Limited

Reprinted 1978 by
Gower Press, Teakfield Limited

Reprinted 1981 by Gower Publishing Company Limited,
Westmead, Farnborough, Hampshire, England

Group training techniques.
   1. Management
   2. Group relations training
   I. Berger, M.L.   II. Berger, P.J.
   658.4'07'1244   HM134

ISBN 0-7161-0102-5

PRINTED IN GREAT BRITAIN

Contents

NOTES ON CONTRIBUTORS   xi

PREFACE   xv

INTRODUCTION   1

PART ONE   GROUP TRAINING APPROACHES   13

1   T-group training, by Peter B Smith   15

     Goals of T-group training   15
     Method of T-group training   16
     How T-groups work   17
     What T-groups achieve   27
     How the T-group atmosphere is created   27
     Evaluating the effects of T-groups   29
     Current developments in T-group training   30

2   Course design and methods within the organisation,
     by Harold Bridger   34

     Organisational self-review and development   35
     Responding to a changing environment   35
     Training in an 'open-system' organisation   37
     Uses of various group-training techniques   38
     Role of the 'appointed leader'   39
     Role of top management   40
     The 'invisible management college'   42
     Designing an internal course   44
     Evaluation of courses   46

3   Managerial Grid training: an application in ICI
     Pharmaceuticals Division, by George Clark   49

     The Grid concept   50
     Grid organisation development   52
     Why ICI chose the Managerial Grid   55
     How the Grid was introduced   57
     Phase 1 experience   58
     Phase 1A projects   59
     Evaluation   60
     Alternative procedures   63
     Guidelines for using Managerial Grid training   64

PART TWO   TRAINING ON-GOING WORK GROUPS   67

4   Building an effective work team, by Iain Mangham   69

     Initial consultant/client interaction   70
     Teamwork development in action   73
     Evaluation   79

5   Role negotiation: a tough-minded approach to team
     development, by Roger Harrison   83

     Stages of a role-negotiation programme   86
     The dynamics of role negotiation   94
     The economics of role negotiation   95
     Summary   96

6   Group training and consultancy approaches in IBM UK Ltd,
     by Alan Drinkwater   98

     Action training   101
     Organisation laboratory   104
     Team-building consultancy   111

PART THREE   RESEARCH ON THE
EFFECTIVENESS OF TRAINING   119

7   The back-home environment and training effectiveness,
     by David Moscow   121

     Technical data from the Leeds research   122
     Results   123
     Relationship of results to existing theory and research findings 125
     Some case studies   129
     Implications for the organisation   130

8   The outcome of a group training course for Ford Motor
Credit Company, by Pamela Berger   134

    The project   135
    Description and results of questionnaires   136
    Summary   143
    General comments about the project   144

9   Selection and training effectiveness, by Mel Berger   147

    Individual and organisational suitability   148
    Are there people who should not attend T-groups?   148
    Which people will learn most from T-groups?   150
    Application of course learning   153
    Guidelines for selecting T-group members   154

PART FOUR   THE TRAINER   157

10   The group leader and training effectiveness,
by Cary L Cooper   159

    Research on trainer influence and participant change   160
    Implications of the research   163

11   A course for training trainers, by Alan Beardon   167

    Planning the course   168
    The first week   169
    The second week   171
    Conclusion   174

GLOSSARY   175

SOME TRAINING CENTRES   181

FURTHER READING   183

INDEX   185

Illustrations

1   Goals and degree of structuring of training approaches   8

1:1   Activities included in a typical T-group training programme   18

2:1   Some differences between closed and open systems   41

3:1   The Managerial Grid describing five principal managerial styles   51

3:2   Model for pnase 2 teamwork development   54

3:3   Member ratings of understanding gained from a phase 1 seminar   60

3:4   Member ratings of application of learning from a phase 1 seminar   61

3:5   Macclesfield site : experience after one year's operation under WSA conditions   62

4:1   Department organisation chart   70

4:2   Extract from questionnaire given to course members   72

4:3   Initial programme for team training   74

5:1   Issue diagnosis form   90

5:2   Summary of messages to James Farrell from other group members   91

5:3   Final written agreement between James Farrell and David Sills   93

7:1   Dimensions of interview scores   124

7:2   Job situation and course learning related to behaviour change on the job six to nine months after the course   126

8:1   Numbers of questionnaires returned   136

8:2   Course members' average scores in five categories of analysis of case study   138

8:3   Number of responses placed in each of the categories of course members' change as reported by course members and their work associates   140

8:4 Examples of responses to change questionnaire 140

8:5 Average number of problems per person by management level reported at the beginning of the course and six months later 143

9:1 Details of the relationship between personal characteristics and subsequent change on the job 153

Notes on contributors

Alan Beardon was educated at Michael Hall Rudolf Steiner School, Lincoln College, Oxford and the Netherlands Industrial Training Institute (NPI) Zeist. He was commissioned into the Royal Artillery during National Service and was a work-camp leader in Austria for UNA's International Service. He has worked as a management trainer for the Steel Company of Wales and Philips Electrical, as a consultant to Esso, and HM Prisons Commission. He is currently a lecturer in Applied Behavioural Science at North London Polytechnic where he does management training.

Mel Berger has been living in England for the past eight years since graduating from the University of California at Los Angeles — BSc in Business Administration, MBA in Behavioural Science. He has since done research in the Management Department of the North London Polytechnic in London. He has considerable experience of group training, both as a trainer and a researcher. At present he is a Research Officer at Birkbeck College and spends most of his time advising and researching management and organisation development in Reed International. He is also involved in management training and in organisational consulting.

Pam Berger graduated from the University of California at Los Angeles with a BSc in psychology. She then completed one year of postgraduate work in clinical psychology at the University of Portland. In 1966 she came to England and was an associate student at the Tavistock Clinic for one year before becoming a research assistant at the North London Polytechnic

Management Department. There she was involved in research and T-group training. At present she is carrying out research for an M Phil in social psychology.

Harold Bridger read mathematics at University College London and, until the beginning of the War, was senior mathematics master at Bablake School Coventry. After commanding a searchlight battery until 1943, he was seconded to the newly set up War Office Selection Boards and was closely associated with the development and use of group methods. He designed and conducted the 'therapeutic community' experiment at Northfield Military Hospital and later joined the technical staff of the Civil Resettlement Units (for returned prisoners of war) as Chief Vocational Officer. He was a founder member of the Tavistock Institute of Human Relations which he joined at its inception in 1946. He qualified as a psycho-analyst in 1950.

Mr Bridger is currently concerned with research and development in group and organisational processes, management career development, and directing the consultation and counselling service of the Tavistock Institute. He recently accepted an invitation to act as a social science adviser to Philips Industries (UK). He is a founder member and Fellow of the European Institute (EIT) for Trans-national Studies in Group and Organis-ational Development, and an Associate Member of the NTL Institute for Applied Behavioural Science of the United States. He is also a member of the Board of the International Institute for Organisational and Social Development (IOD). He wrote Psycho-dynamics of Inter-group Experience (Tavistock 1965).

George Clark graduated BSc in pharmacy from Manchester University in 1944 and is a Fellow of the Pharmaceutical Society of Great Britain. He joined ICI in 1945 and spent nine years on research and development followed by three years in charge of overseas technical work for the Pharmaceuticals Division. In 1957 he joined the Works organisation becoming Works Manager in charge of the manufacture of fermentation products. With the introduction of new ideas for more effective utilisation of manpower (later the Weekly Staff Agreement) he was appointed the Pharmaceuticals Division Coordinator for this work and a member of the ICI central steering committee. In 1968 he became manager of the newly created Training Development Department of the Pharmaceuticals Division, combining overall responsibility for training the Division's employees with organisation development and a consultancy group for the effective use of human resources. He is a member of an advisory council at Manchester University which reviews the syllabus for the postgraduate diploma in Industrial Education and Training.

Cary L Cooper graduated from the University of California, Los Angeles in 1962 and obtained a Master's degree in behavioural science from the same university in 1964. He obtained a PhD at the University of Leeds, the work for which was carried out in the Department of Management Studies at the University of Leeds and the Department of Social Psychology at the University of Sussex. He is currently Lecturer in Social Psychology at the University of Southampton where he teaches and researches into small-group behaviour. He has co-edited a book on T-group research for John Wiley & Sons.

Alan Drinkwater is a Management Development Officer within the Central Personnel Department of IBM (UK) Limited. He regards himself as a 'personnel man'. Having graduated in geography and worked in the steel industry he decided, relatively late, to develop his career in personnel management. He enrolled on the one-year diploma course at the London School of Economics, then worked for Esso Petroleum Company Limited as a recruiter and for Colgate-Palmolive Limited as a personnel 'generalist'. He joined IBM two years ago and since then he has been involved in the design and running of training activities for supervisors and managers. More recently he has been engaged in consultancy activities with groups of managers in three of the Company's divisions.

Roger Harrison is Vice President and London Representative of Development Research Associates, Inc., a firm of applied behavioural scientists specialising in management training and organisational develop- ment. A social psychologist by training, Dr Harrison gained early experience as a personnel researcher with the Procter and Gamble Company and then taught for a number of years in the Department of Industrial Administration and the Department of Psychology at Yale University. He is a Fellow of the NTL Institute of Applied Behavioural Science and has written numerous papers on the evaluation of management training, the design of learning experiences, and the theory and practice of organisational change.

Iain Mangham has a degree in sociology and has recently completed work for a PhD in psychology. He has been involved in applied behavioural science since his early work in the theatre and education, but on a more formal level since 1965. He has been Deputy Director of the Department of Management Studies and Head of the Organisation Development Unit at the University of Leeds. He has written several articles, one book on T-group research with Cary Cooper and has another in preparation on organisation development with John Adams. He acts as Personnel and Organisation Development Consultant to a number of large British and American companies. He is currently an area director for Eli Lilly International Corporation, responsible for organisation and training, and development issues within Italy, Southern Europe, Middle East and North Africa.

David Moscow is currently working in his own consulting management firm, Sheppard, Moscow and Associates. He graduated in sociology and social psychology at the University of Leicester in 1959, then worked in the civil engineering and aircraft industries as a personnel officer. He first became involved with T-group training in 1963 at the University of Leeds, where he was a lecturer in social psychology in the Department of Management Studies. He moved to Holland in 1967 as a research associate at the Netherlands Institute for Preventive Medicine, Leiden, Holland. There he conducted research on T-groups and management consulting.

He is a member of the Group Relations Training Association in Britain, the Dutch Trainers Association and EIT (European Institute for Transnational Studies in Group and Organisational Development) and has conducted T-groups for industrial and educational establishments in Britain and the USA.

Peter B Smith is Lecturer in Social Psychology at the University of Sussex. Graduating in psychology at the University of Cambridge in 1959, he remained there to undertake research. His PhD was concerned with the differentiation of roles among discussion groups on management training programmes. He became interested in the potentialities of T-group training methods and moved to the Department of Management Studies at Leeds University, where these methods were an active focus of interest. He moved to Sussex in 1966. During the past eight years he has conducted research into the effectiveness and mechanism of T-group training, and has conducted T-groups for a wide variety of managers, students, social workers and teachers.

He edited Group Processes (Penguin Books).

Preface

Group training has increasingly become accepted as important to the development of man-management skills. Nowadays most managers know about some group training approaches but few know of the full range, the differences between them, how they could be applied and whether, in fact, they would be appropriate for their organisation. Group training approaches are being modified and invented quite regularly these days and each is given a new name: group relations training, Managerial Grid, T-group training, organisation development, Coverdale training, team training, study groups, action training, sensitivity training, organisation laboratory and many more.

Most books on group training tend to specialise in one particular approach and are often highly technical. The purpose of this book is to introduce the reader to some of the major group training approaches, to illustrate how organisations have used the approach, to describe some recent research concerned with increasing training effectiveness, and to provide guidelines for the implementation of group training. However, it is emphasised that group training skills cannot be acquired from reading alone and this book is not intended to teach people how to train groups.

The book is intended to be readily understandable and of practical use to people interested in the use of group training or who work with groups, be they managers, trainers, or educators. Hence, there was a strong desire to minimise the use of highly technical language. To the extent that this was not possible, a glossary is provided at the end.

The material is organised as a series of articles written by experienced practitioners currently working in Britain. There is a comprehensive introduction which provides an overview and introduces the reader to some basic definitions. Reading the first two chapters will provide some theoretical background and rationale for group training. Subsequent chapters describe specific approaches or research studies.

We should like to acknowledge the considerable help we received in planning the book from our friend, John Searle, and the valuable criticisms from Mary Jane and Peter Spink, Elizabeth Glead, Mike Simmons, David Casey and Peter Smith.

M. B.
P. J. B.

Introduction

In recent years there has been a growing interest in the human aspects of management. Man-management skills such as group decision-making, motivation, communication between people, and interviewing are seen as making an important contribution to organisational success. This has led to the introduction of training, often called either human relations training or group dynamics training, specifically aimed at helping managers to improve these skills. The teaching approach varies considerably, from case studies and role playing to simulated work situations and T-group training.

This book is about a variety of approaches to man-management training called group training. Group training differs from more traditional approaches, such as lecturing, case studies and role playing, in two basic ways.

First, the training aims to improve the skills of group members by focusing on the training group itself. That is, problems which arise out of the experience of working together in the training group are examined with the aim of improving the group's effectiveness or the individual's effectiveness as a member of the group. Thus, people learn by their own experience; this is sometimes called experiential learning.

In contrast, a case study or a role play involves a situation which is either fictional, historical, or real to someone other than the trainees. In some cases people pretend and act out a character in the case. In group training, the group is its own on-going case study and people are themselves.

Second, in group training considerable emphasis is placed on evaluating the performance of the individual and/or the group. This generally leads to experimenting with new behaviours and new styles of working in the group.

The original form of group training is the T-group ('T' stands for training), also called sensitivity training, laboratory training or group relations training. It originated about twenty-five years ago and has developed and grown at an increasing rate. Although first developed in the United States, its use in Britain extends back almost as long as in the States. Over the years, T-group training has become very diverse and has led to a variety of more specialised group training approaches.

One of the unique features of the 'classical' T-group is that the trainer does not overtly take the leadership role or structure the group sessions. (By structure is meant explicit procedures, rules and leadership.) This results in the group having to evolve its own structure. Also, course members generally are trained in isolation from their day-to-day work associates. Variations on the original T-group are often structured by the trainer and members may be managers of the same organisation, even the same work group. This trend has led to what is called organisation development or OD.

OD is an approach for encouraging exploration and planned development of managerial group and organisational processes. It involves the use of behavioural science knowledge and generally originates near the top of the organisation. Whereas management development aims at developing the skills of managers so that they may contribute more to the organisation, OD aims to create an environment which will facilitate effective contributions to the organisation. Thus OD focuses on groups, work relationships, inter-group relations, target- and goal-setting and planning.

There are related approaches to group training which focus on the individual himself, usually called 'encounter groups'. These groups generally centre around each participant in turn who wishes to work on a particular problem in his life.

People attend these for their own personal growth and they often have a therapeutic flavour. Their goal is to increase personal competence without reference to organisational effectiveness, although there may be a spin-off to organisational settings. As they are seldom directly used in organisations, they will not be described in this book.

Group training has been applied to help organisations in several different ways. Some organisations regularly send managers to group training courses composed of individuals from various organisations; these are called 'stranger' groups. They have also been used within organisations; these are called 'in company' groups. In-company training may include a complete work team; this is called a 'family' group or team training. Alternatively, people from the same organisation who do not work closely with one another may be trained together, this is called a 'cousins' group. 'Stranger', 'cousins' and 'family' groups differ in several respects. In a stranger group relationships are temporary, lasting only as long as the course. This usually makes it easier for members to question their normal style of behaviour and to experiment with different styles of working in groups. On the other hand, what is learned has to be adapted to the job setting among people who may not have been on the same or a similar course. This may lead to suspicion and resistance if the returning manager attempts to introduce change or indeed to behave differently himself. In a family group, the relationship between group members has both a history and a future. The risks from self-assessment and experimentation are thus higher than with strangers. In this situation, the training course is likely to be less personal and more related to work relationships and work problems. What is learned, though it may be less deep than from a stranger course, has a greater likelihood of being transferred to the work situation. A cousins group represents an intermediate position, involving more risk than a stranger group and less than a family group.

The book is organised into four parts. The first part presents three different basic group training approaches, from the relatively unstructured T-group to a highly structured training package called the Managerial Grid.

Part Two describes three team-building or OD consultancy approaches. The third part considers several research studies on the effectiveness of training. Part Four focuses on the trainer's effect on the training outcome and presents an example of a training for trainers course.

In Part One, three basic group training approaches are presented : the T-group, a structured training method, and in-company training. Besides describing the approach, each chapter provides an illustration of its use.

The opening chapter, by Peter Smith, elaborates the nature and methods of the T-group, discusses how it differs from traditional approaches, and presents excerpts from the life of one particular T-group. It lays the groundwork for later specialised topics and case material. Smith sees the T-group goals as helping people to increase their ability to :

1   Sense accurately the reactions of others to their behaviour
2   Sum up accurately the behaviour of others and of groups
3   Behave appropriately and effectively in various interpersonal situations

It sets out to achieve these goals primarily by studying the behaviour of the group members themselves. In this way, course members may learn about different ways of communicating, making decisions, handling conflicts in groups, obtaining cooperation, as well as developing an awareness of themselves and their impact on other group members and on the performance of the group itself. For example, particular styles of leadership may be found to have certain consequences in terms of group involvement, motivation and effectiveness. The group is encouraged to adopt an approach which emphasises periodic monitoring of group and individual performance and experimentation with new approaches to working in groups.

In Chapter 2, Harold Bridger presents a stimulating discussion of the problems with which organisations are increasingly faced in a changing world and the use of group training to deal with these problems. The increased rate of technological, economic and social change results in uncertainty, complexity and interdependence of roles and functions within the organisation. From this trend the need arises for organisations to become more 'open' systems, that is, to be more interactive with and responsive to both the external environment and to the various internal functions, such as sales, production and research. The role for management in an open-system organisation places great emphasis on managing the boundaries between functions or departments and between the organisation and its environment. The manager's world is one of multi-accountability : to the unit's environment, to colleagues, superiors, central administration and other functions. With regard to his subordinates, his primary task is that of climate-setting, based on shared responsibility, which implies both a common goal and whole tasks. His leader role is made more complex by the fact that some of his subordinates may be accountable to the manager's superiors and colleagues as well as to himself.

Although many people would agree that these changes are necessary, Bridger points out that it is nonetheless very difficult for them to 'unlearn' traditional methods, assumptions and standards. This often results in introducing new, glossy management techniques in an effort to sort things out, rather than in developing people's capabilities and skills to cope with a new organisational role. He feels that it is important for managers to take time out to think through organisational objectives, structural options, and conflicting role relationships. They must be able to understand why problems arise in the first place, and to examine the assumptions and values which underlie their procedures and performance. They must be free to try out new approaches and to evaluate their effectiveness.

Group training can help managers to develop required skills and to test their assumptions in a relatively safe setting. Courses of all kinds can spend time looking at the organisational processes and sub-cultures of the course itself; in essence the course becomes an open-system organisation. However important courses may be, they are no substitute for on-the-job learning and training. Courses can accelerate the organisation development process but to do so they must be part of an overall organisation development plan and they must be integrated into the manager's job situation through pre-course and follow-up discussions with work associates. Specific benefits of in-company group training include giving managers the opportunity to understand how they behave when engaged in task work, to try out new methods of behaviour, to discuss man-management work problems and to develop cross-functional and cross-cultural awareness and understanding.

Chapter 3, by George Clark, describes a specific, highly structured training approach called the 'Managerial Grid', developed by Blake and Mouton. The first of six phases of Grid training is aimed at educating the manager about the Grid approach including working in groups effectively, facilitating interaction between groups, and understanding the effect of various managerial styles. The further phases apply the Grid technique to on-going groups. Clark describes how the ICI Pharmaceuticals Division used phase 1 to aid the implementing of an agreement between the company and the unions. He concludes that the training played a considerable part in the division exceeding their manning and financial targets and reducing labour turnover. However, he felt that the benefits of the training could have been increased much further had phase 2 been implemented with family groups to facilitate application of learning.

Part Two deals with training on-going work units or family groups. In this type of training, the trainer is usually a consultant whose contact with the organisation is more long term than a single course. He is generally involved in preparation before the course, such as interviewing members, and in follow-up meetings. The course is often structured around specific work problems or work relationships.

Chapter 4 by Iain Mangham presents an example of training for team building. The aim of the training was to raise the effectiveness of the work team through increasing personal involvement, increasing openness, and gaining commitment to continual review of performance. The course consisted of a series of exercises and discussions designed to reveal how group members saw the group, to identify how they would ideally like the group to be, and to come up with methods which would improve the working of the group. A modified version of MBO (Management by Objectives) was also set up during the course. Subsequently, top management felt that the objectives were met and that morale had improved.

Chapter 5 by Roger Harrison describes a new and exciting approach developed by the author, called role negotiation. The technique involves each team member considering the other team members in terms of what they would like that person to do more of or do better, do less of, and continue doing as present. The changes desired should be ones that the person feels will increase his own performance effectiveness. They are written down and form the basis of negotiation which in turn involves group members in bargaining and reaching agreements to make reciprocal changes. The technique differs markedly from most other group training approaches in that it deals directly with power and influence and in that it aims to manage conflict by negotiation rather than reduce it by building trust, sharing feelings or increasing participation.

Alan Drinkwater's contribution (Chapter 6) describes how the Central Management Development Department of IBM United Kingdom Limited has evolved a team consultation approach in response to what it saw as short-comings of cousin groups. Following dissatisfaction with the usefulness of in-company T-group training, a course called 'action training' was developed which focused on skills of appraisal and counselling, and working in groups. Subsequently, a course called an 'organisation laboratory' was developed to improve skills of building collaborative relationships between groups in an organisation. However, evaluation studies of course usefulness concluded that managers often found it difficult to implement what they had learned from these courses. To overcome this problem, the Department made itself available to consult with on-going work groups. This usually involves a trainer taking part in a number of work meetings to help the group improve its method of work, interviewing group members to find out their views about group problems, and arranging special meetings to sort out these problems. This approach is sometimes called process consultancy in that consultation is concerned with the process of the group's work rather than with technical or task problems. Currently, the Central Management Development Department is involved in both group training and consultancy.

T-group training has stimulated a considerable amount of research — more than most other training methods. Part Three presents some recent research studies which cast light on how the job setting affects a member's change on the job and the selection of course members. Though based on T-groups, these studies also have general relevance to other types of group training and to education.

David Moscow's article (Chapter 7) considers participant learning from the point of view of the man's work climate and work relationships. He reports the research he conducted and provides case studies illustrating the process of transferring course learning to the job. From pre-course interviews, trainees' work climates and work relationships were categorised as either good, moderate or poor. It was found that those participants who had either a good or a poor work climate and a good or poor relationship to their boss did not change on the job following the course to the same extent as those who had a moderate work climate and a moderate relationship to their boss. Moscow explains that those with good relationships 'would not have much encouragement to change' and that those with difficult work relationships, although they often showed considerable course learning, 'are likely to find that the work changes they make during training are either not in line with, or inadequately meet, the expectations of their work associates, particularly their boss. '

Chapter 9 considers whether some trainees are likely to learn more than others in T-groups and whether some people should not attend them at all. There is controversy over whether the only people who benefit from T-groups are those who least need it because they already are highly skilled in dealing with people — or whether a wide variety of different types of people can benefit from T-groups. This was tested by comparing learning of members with 'democratic' values with learning of members with 'autocratic' values. Given the nature of the T-group, it was assumed that members with 'autocratic' values had more to learn from the experience than members with 'democratic' values. It was found that 'autocratic' members learned more that 'democratic' members in two-week groups but the reverse was true in one-week groups. 'Autocratic' managers are more confronted and challenged by the T-group and therefore have potentially more to gain from it than 'democratic' managers. However, one week is likely to be too short to realise this potential while two weeks are generally sufficient. The conclusion is that those who have most to gain from T-groups often do so, but only if the course lasts two weeks. The chapter also includes some guidelines for deciding whether some people should not be sent on T-groups. Though this is a small minority of people, their identification is important.

Together, Chapters 7 and 9 provide selection guidelines for the training officer or manager with responsibility for management development. They imply that organisational work relationships should be monitored, that a single training course, in and of itself, is not sufficient to change poor work relationships, and that the individual's management style and development needs should be matched with the types of courses available.

Chapter 8 discusses the result of a cousins training course in terms of learning and subsequent job behaviour. The aim of the course run for Ford Motor Credit Company was to improve managerial skills of communication and working in groups. The research was based on questionnaires, completed by the course member, his boss, and one subordinate before and six months after the course. The training course led to job behaviour change in half of the members. However, some of the learning diminished in the six months following the course and some new problems arose between the trained managers and their bosses. To an extent this is an inevitable and often ultimately beneficial consequence of training. If the gap between training goals and current organisation standards and practices is too great, the training is not likely to be useful and may even increase frustration and discontent among those who have been trained. In this case the gap was not so wide as to prevent a substantial amount of behaviour change on the job by trainees. The learning probably would have been greater had the training been extended to more than one level of management, or had follow-up support been provided to trainees. This could have taken the form of further group meetings, individual consultation, team training or multi-level problem-solving meetings.

The degree to which the group achieves its potential depends, to a large extent, on the trainer's skills. Part Four focuses on the trainer. Cary Cooper, in Chapter 10, discusses the trainer's position and concludes that the way the trainer is perceived by group members has a major impact on learning.

Trainers who are seen as trustworthy, self-disclosing, and genuine with group members foster relationships which are most likely to lead to learning which can be transferred to the job. On the other hand, members who come to identify with and depend on the trainer for cues about how to behave in the group, are likely to change during the course but often do not transfer this learning to the back-home environment. The trainer's behaviour is critical in determining whether his relationship to participants is based on genuineness or on dependency. It is therefore important that trainers be carefully selected and trained. Like other highly skilled jobs, some people have greater aptitude than others and, in all cases, considerable training is necessary. Although these conclusions were based on research of T-group trainers, they apply to structured group training approaches as well, though probably to a somewhat lesser extent. In general, the more unstructured the approach, the more skills a trainer must have. This point is discussed in Chapters 2 and 5.

A course designed to help develop T-group trainers and to teach industrial trainers the use of group training techniques is described by Alan Beardon. It was aimed at people with previous T-group and practical training experience. The course mainly consisted of a T-group, structured exercises and the task of planning and running a one-day course for students. This task provided the participants with a real training situation to cope with under the supervision of experienced trainers.

In all, a wide variety of group training approaches are presented in the book. It would be useful to examine them in a systematic way. Figure 1 shows the training approaches described in relation to goals and structure. The training goal for team training and some cousins groups was organisation development. The goal for stranger and some cousins groups was developing managerial skills. The chart shows that where an on-going work unit is involved, the approach is generally more structured than where strangers are involved. There are exceptions to this trend, but they are not described in this book.

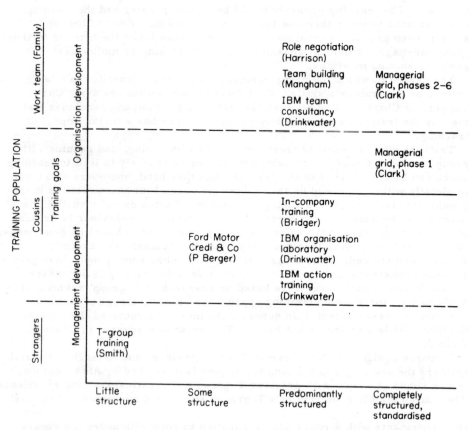

Figure 1   Goals and degree of structuring of training approaches

The chapters describing the approaches used by various organisations point to the need for considerable planning and preparation before setting up a programme of group training. This undoubtedly applies to introducing any new techniques. Some general guidelines are set out below.

Preparation of a training programme

It can take a good deal of time to plan and prepare a training or development programme. The first step is to diagnose development needs, preferably by discussion with the people who will be involved in the programme. From this it will be possible to set specific objectives. For example, the objective may be to change existing management practices, to train new managers, to increase the efficiency of group decision-making, or to improve communication.

It is important to obtain commitment from as high a level in the organisation as possible. Commitment from top management may be gained by maintaining a close liaison with them throughout the programme, by encouraging them to go on a stranger course in order to find out for themselves the benefits of the training, or by setting up a pilot course or discussion day just for them. These two steps, if successful, should lead to involvement and commitment of those who will take part and to support from where it is needed most. This, in turn, will increase the likelihood of the success of the overall programme.

Follow-up on the job

Although courses are the usual first step in improving managerial skill, follow-up with on-going work units is important in order to gain maximum benefits. Without follow-up, managers may encounter difficulties in implementing new ideas and in changing their approach because of lack of support by their work associates or fear of trying new things or because of lack of confidence in their own expertise. Follow-up, even on a voluntary basis, ensures that managers or work units who desire to make changes will get sufficient help and guidance. This may take the form of team training, process consultancy, or project work.

An organisation development sequence

Some organisations have developed an overall OD sequence. Initially, top managers may go to stranger groups in order to sample group training approaches. The company then may run a series of cousin courses aimed at introducing new ideas, techniques, man-management approaches, and a common language. From this, managers may feel that training their family group would be useful.

Family group training is most likely to succeed if most of the members have had a previous group experience. Although it is usually helpful to have outside expert advice in the early stages of the programme, it may be more economical and often more effective to train people inside the company to conduct the actual training programmes. In some cases, it has been found useful to have one or two external consultants who work with the internal trainers or consultants on a regular basis. The training of internal trainers does require both time and money. Often, this involves sending them on external courses, such as T-groups or OD training groups, in order that they learn basic skills of working in groups, increase their understanding of group processes, and learn in depth the impact they have on others. Some organisations have set up in-company trainer development programmes.

Training should fit the organisation

The training approach should not be too dissimilar from the existing organisational climate and structure. Organisations in environments which are relatively unpredictable and changeable usually have the greatest need for group training. These organisations cannot rely on standard procedures and must be able to make good decisions at all managerial levels based on specialist information and on changing circumstances. An organisation which is rigidly structured and which has fairly fixed well-defined procedures would probably find a highly structured training approach more acceptable to the individuals involved. On the other hand, an organisation with flexible structure and procedures would probably find a moderately structured approach most acceptable.

Where the training approach is not seen as acceptable to trainees, regardless of its 'objective' merits, there is likely to be considerable resistance to the programme. Since group training involves people and the complexities of human nature, without goodwill and commitment, resistance is likely and this will greatly reduce the learning potential of the programme.

Selection

Training will be most successful where client organisations take responsibility for careful selection, preparation and follow-up of potential group members and where training organisations take responsibility for selecting and training trainers.

Evaluation

Periodic monitoring of the training programme is advisable to ensure that the development objectives are being met. This may necessitate experimentation with slightly different training approaches.

Need for research

The research evidence to support the above conclusions and guidelines is far from complete. Careful planning and cooperation between organisations undergoing training, trainers, and researchers is necessary in order to increase the long-term effectiveness of training and organisation development.

M. B.

PART ONE

GROUP TRAINING APPROACHES

T-group training

by Peter B Smith

T-group training comprises a situation where trainees meet for the purpose of communicating directly with one another about how they see each other's behaviour. Such a procedure constitutes a decidedly novel approach and is one which has at different times evoked both enthusiasm and suspicion. 'T-group' is an abbreviation for Training group, thus making the whole phrase peculiarly uninformative. One advantage of the unusual name is that it successfully communicates that the method is something markedly different from more familiar training methods.

The goals and methods of T-group training will be reviewed first, then, more briefly, some reasons why the method might be effective, the evidence on whether it is effective and current applications of the method in this country.

GOALS OF T-GROUP TRAINING

The goals of T-group training can be placed under three general headings:

1   An increase in <u>sensitivity</u>, in other words, the ability to sense accurately the reactions of others to one's own behaviour
2   An increase in <u>diagnostic ability</u>, in other words the ability to sum up accurately the behaviour going on between others
3   An increase in <u>action skill</u>, by which is meant the ability to select and

perform in a skilled manner whatever behaviour the situation calls for

These goals are expressed in generalised and abstract terms, whose relevance to the world of the industrial manager may not be immediately apparent. The specific goals of a group depend more on the particular population in training. For example, trainers would have quite different goals in mind for a group consisting of managers drawn from a range of different companies (a 'stranger' group) than they would for a group comprising an intact organisational work team, or for a group who, although not a work team, are all employed by the same organisation.

METHOD OF T-GROUP TRAINING

There is a central core of method which constitutes the fundamental difference between T-group and other training developments.
    The T-group may be compared with the discussion of case studies in human relations. In the T-group the focus is on those present. The trainer encourages the group members to observe the behaviour of each of the members of the group. He indicates that, by sharing their observations, members can check whether they see events in the group the same way that others do. Where they disagree, further observations can be made. In a case study, by contrast, only a single source of data is available and dis-agreements about how to interpret it are frequently soluble only by members deciding arbitrarily to accept one interpretation as the correct one.
    In the T-group, one is not only an observer of the group's behaviour, one also participates in it and has the potentiality of influencing what happens next. If a particular topic or procedure is mooted, one may agree, disagree remain silent or propose something else. ('I think we should all say what first impressions we have formed of one another.' 'I disagree; we do not have enough to go on — let's describe some things about the jobs we do.') Skill in human relations consists in a judicious mixture of observing and participating, and the T-group demands just such a mixture. In contrast, a case study stresses heavily the observation or diagnosis element.
    In the T-group, the focus is on telling each member how his behaviour affects the others in the group. The trainer encourages members to say how they felt when the individual behaved in a particular way. ('What you said came over very clearly; I was very pleased — at last someone was beginning to talk some sense.' 'I wasn't listening — you go on so much that I'd given up.') The rationale for this procedure is that each individual can then examine whether he is creating the effects on others that he would hope for. Our goals vary but each of us needs feedback to see whether or not we are achieving them. This procedure again contrasts markedly with a case study where the emphasis is on advice rather than feedback. Most T-groups pass through a period of advice-giving ('you ought to talk more; it's too easy just to sit and watch us flounder') but they discover sooner or later that it is not very productive. When someone receives advice, the only basis on which

he can decide to accept or reject it is the quality of his relationship with the giver of the advice. If the giver spells out his reasons for giving the advice it becomes more like feedback ('When you sit quiet, I feel uncomfortable') and the receiver has some concrete data to work on. If he doesn't mind whether the giver feels uncomfortable or not, he will remain quiet; if he does, he may spell out his own feelings.

HOW T-GROUPS WORK

The progress made by different T-groups toward this rather distinctive set of procedures is varied. A great deal depends on the trainees and the nature of their goals, expectations and anxieties. The development of a particular T-group is illustrated by reference to some quotations from tape recordings of a 'stranger' group held some years ago in the UK. It was composed of middle managers and two trainers. The quotations form a sequence from early sessions to late sessions during training. The training programme was residential and lasted ten days. While all the quotations are drawn from the meetings of a single T-group, it is usual for a T-group training programme to include a variety of activities other than T-group meetings. Some of the most typical of these are listed in Figure 1:1. As can be seen many of these are designed to augment or extend the trainee's experience in his T-group.

The quotations focus solely on the T-group. They were selected randomly with the exception of the first one. Consequently, they illustrate average activities of the group, not particularly significant or crucial episodes. Each quotation is fairly brief and the session of the group from which it is drawn is indicated. In reading through the sequence one can discern a number of developmental trends. For example, the focus of the early interchanges is on how the group should proceed, or on problems encountered by group members in their jobs. The only references to the actual situation within the T-group are expressions of difficulty or fears of what may happen. Later sessions are given over to discussion of each person's reaction to others in the group. The group evidently becomes a more cohesive unit, and some changes are apparent in the trainers' roles. Initially their contributions are markedly different from those of the trainees, but this difference is much reduced in the later sessions. The trainer's behaviour is as much a topic for scrutiny as anyone else's. The total time this group spent in discussion with one another was approximately 40 hours.

Session 1

In the first session, we find several group members trying to persuade one of the two trainers to give them a more specific lead on what to talk about:

Tom. Do you find this sort of thing develops better when somebody comes out with a set topic, or when there is a semi-aimless discussion?

17

Element	Purpose
Lectures	Intellectual clarification of problems in group and organisational behaviour
Intergroup observation	To see similarities and differences in the ways different groups face up to common issues
Paired discussion	Practice: (i) in helping someone else to obtain benefit from his T-group; (ii) in receiving such help
Non-verbal exercises	Extension of T-group to examine interpersonal communication other than by word of mouth
Intergroup exercises	Extension of T-group learning to problems of representation, negotiation and conflict management
Application groups	To facilitate the transfer of what has been learned to the trainee's actual job behaviour
Group recomposition	To bring together trainees who may be particularly able to learn from one another
Research data collection	Monitoring the success of the laboratory, plus making a contribution to long-term development of the method

Figure 1:1   Activities included in a typical T-group training programme

Jim (trainer). I don't think a topic helps very much.
Tom.   No, I noticed that with the group, when they got on to about the only concrete topic, for instance the behaviour of board meetings, the discussion was far more of a semi-technical nature than of a personal nature, and everybody was edging round.
Alf.   That's because the situation was recognisable to them, I think.
Tom.   Yes, whilst it was more interesting getting the discussion sparking off, it wasn't achieving what I think we are trying to achieve, but I am not quite sure what that is.
Dick.   Topics, I suppose, in your terms, tend to detract from what you call the 'here and now' situation, would that be the case?
Jim (trainer).   Yes, it is a lot more comfortable to talk about abstractions, about people who are not here, about situations outside of this room. These are all kinds of escapes from facing the problem that I see we have to face

here, which is how do we go about the task of really learning about each other, about becoming a real group.

Session 2

The second session shows the group in an abstract discussion of the process of giving 'feedback', which is telling another person how one reacts to something he has done. The trainer is encouraging the group to try it out but group members express fears about what might happen if one did that on the job. They evidently still find it difficult to focus on their own group.

Dick. If you are using feedback, it must be of mutual use — am I right in thinking?
Tom. Yes, it could be very dangerous using it on somebody who had not been on one of these courses.
Jim (trainer). It is not always a subordinate/boss relationship though, is it? You drew me out on that point, which is quite a valid one. You often find yourselves in a situation where you have to deal with other people who of their own right are in a completely free situation. They don't have to take any notice of you at all, and you have got to be careful about treading on their toes as well as on your boss's toes.
Mary. But why are we so afraid to do this is a point which came out — I think Bill was saying something to the effect that if we did this we might get chopped ourselves, and this is why we didn't.
Bill. Yes, I did.
Mary. And this is our reason. It is not so much what they may think of us but what they might do to us. In other words, it is our restriction rather than anything they are imposing on us which prevents us from saying what we really think, perhaps.
Bill. Well, it is only the restriction that is put upon us by our experience perhaps of having done this, and when you have experienced this once, and have been chopped down, you are not inclined to do it a second time. If you knew your boss was aware that this was a useful technique so that you were sort of feeding back madly to one another, and chopping one another down to size and enjoying the whole thing, that would be all right wouldn't it?
Jim (trainer). We don't have any bosses in this room, fortunately, so we are here really just as a group of people. We may never see each other again after these two weeks, so presumably this would be a good experimental arena in which we could try out ways of behaving that we would be reluctant to try out when with our bosses.

Session 3

In this session, the excerpt consists of a single, somewhat confused reflection by one group member on the effect of the group on him. It has set him thinking about his style as a manager in a general way without giving him any specific learning so far.

Dick. Well, for example, one of the things that flashed through my mind this morning was that although the conversations, I am talking about the very first session, were without any purpose, one thing that I rather concluded was that one does get some useful summed result when the group takes part in considering a situation. That happened rather surprisingly when the situation was completely loose, and wide open, and nobody was talking about anything in particular. I felt something, somewhere, developed out of it. From that it occurred to me that in the jobs which we all do, we are trying to get the best result all the time, the best overall result in any given situation. I have been thinking that the way to do this is to try to get everybody in the organisation to make his contribution to that overall progress, and therefore, the way to do this is to create a climate in that organisation where people feel free to express their opinions. It was also mentioned that if the boss is there, that inhibits you straight away, because you tend to worry about what he thinks you ought to say rather than what you feel ought to be said in the circumstances.

Session 4

By session 4, the group are still 'waiting to begin', but the fears expressed by group members are a lot more specific. Each member has thought through what he fears may happen in the group, and feels free enough to talk about it.

Bill. I have certainly been ... let me put it this way, I have been waiting for the unpleasantness to start, and I think one or two in the other room have had this in mind, that the thing will start to form, it will start to show its purpose when one person starts challenging another and questioning his behaviour, perhaps even riling him a little bit. I suppose this is what I have had in my mind too.
Joe. Well, I have heard from a couple of people who say that if you are a manager, you must expect a lot of trouble with people. Well, as a person who doesn't expect trouble, who doesn't even like trouble, I don't like unpleasantness, I don't look forward to it. Therefore what other people told me I accept as their interpretation.

Session 5

In session 5, we find a similar interchange, with the second trainer encouraging a group member to explore what it is that he feels apprehensive about.

John (trainer). What is it for you Tom that is embarrassing?
Tom. Well, I am probably expressing myself badly, but one is less guarded if one has a drink or two, the defence mechanism drops more.
John (trainer). Are you implying that in this situation at the moment you feel guarded?

__Tom.__   Well, I think most people are feeling a little bit guarded. Well, I feel not exactly apprehensive, but a little bit guarded.

__John (trainer).__   Could you tell me more about what it is you feel guarded about?

__Tom.__   I have put my foot in it now!   (General laughter)

__Dick.__   Could you re-phrase that?

__John (trainer).__   Well, I am interested in knowing ... hearing more from you about what it is you feel guarded about. By guarded, I suppose one usually means that there are things that one could say or feel might be useful, but one guards against saying them.

__Tom.__   Well, I have probably expressed this badly, but I feel rather like — I hate to go back to this again — Dick felt, that if one says too much, one becomes the centre of the group, and one doesn't feel very comfortable being the centre of the group.

Session 8

From now on, excerpts will not be taken from every session as the group settles down to more established procedures. In session 8, Dick, in contrast with the earlier sessions where conversation focused more on the difficulties or dangers of being open with one another, wants to express himself more openly and is seeking advice. We also find a member checking the accuracy of communication in the group by a simple feedback of what he had understood from what was said.

__Dick.__   For someone who has been through the phases I have, what do you suggest I should do to try to unleash my real feelings again? Is there any way of doing this that you know of?

__Jim (trainer).__   One thing is in this group, whenever you feel something, make a point of expressing it. You may discover that the expression of feelings doesn't have as much hurt in it as you suspect. People are a lot tougher than most of us give them credit for being. I would think this is a generalisation.

__Dick.__   Yes, I think this is true, and I think this point of not forming a conclusion in expressing your feelings is very vital too, isn't it? I think I have probably been guilty of that very much in the past, and this has not helped.

__Joe.__   I think it is some form of defence mechanism again, isn't it? I think if you form a hasty opinion or judgement of people, it is a form of defence mechanism.

__Dick.__   I am sorry I am not quite with you. I mean, I can see what you just said, but not quite sure how it relates to the previous things.

__Joe.__   Well, I thought that this is what you said. That is how what you said came across to me.

Session 10

In the next session, there is a brief excerpt from a long interchange between some of the line managers in the group, and two management teachers. Although this difference is probably affecting what is happening in the T-group, at this particular point the group are not succeeding in tackling the question in terms of Joe's relations with Bill, but are talking in more general terms.

Bill. Joe, can I respond at once to this and say that the message that is coming across to me, rightly or wrongly, in this, is that the intellectual or academic, whether he does a good job or a lousy job, gets paid for it, and this is not fair.

Joe. No, I don't think it can be done any other way. I don't think there is a way you can judge this, I think this is just a fact of life. This is the same as the person in the armed forces. To a very large degree the number of people vitally involved in this particular sphere of activity, vitally concerned, are few. You know to replace a teacher, to sack a teacher, is quite a difficult thing to do. You can't get rid of a teacher just because you think he is no good; a principal cannot do these things, it is not so easy, everything is on the line.

Andrew. Is this because there is no yardstick to measure them by?

Joe. Well, there isn't, is there?

Dick. I would like to know how Joe feels about the situation.

Joe. I feel that this is the way the thing is; I have no deep feelings in this. What I feel is that for these people, because the pressure is off instead of having these veneers or barriers, they can be freer to contribute more because they haven't got these pressures.

Session 12

In the next session, the group are discussing Dick's behaviour with him.

Jim (trainer). I get this kind of a feeling too from you, that you are maybe more of a responder, a reactor to what is out there than a guy who is initiating. Is this what you feel, Dick?

Dick. Yes, well, I think this is right really. I think I consciously try and not let my unaided conclusion rule what I do.

Jim (trainer). I wonder why; are you afraid of what might happen if you let yourself go?

Dick. No, not really, it isn't that. As far as I can tell myself, it's because I think if you involve people in the action, they work better at it. I had rather strong tendencies in this regard myself at one time. If it wasn't my idea, I lost all interest in it, but obviously, when you think of this in the round, it is a bad thing. If the idea is only that one person's idea, it means that the ten others involved in the carrying out of it aren't really concerned in it.

Jim (trainer). Yes, I think to some extent this is true. But there is another side of this coin, which is I think also worth looking at, and that is what you are interested in, to get people to link their energies together to get a job done. OK, now one thing that happens is that people are more likely to want to link their energies to somebody who has made a commitment, rather than to somebody who feels neutral. I can see your point, if you go in and say, 'Hey fellas, I've got a great idea that I would like you all to carry out, ' this is not necessarily going to get people excited about things, but I think you don't have to go to the other extreme and say, 'You know, here is a kind of an idea and you know sort of, if we want to look at it we can look at it and so forth. ' I think it is possible to express one's own commitment and interest without necessarily depriving other people of the desire to help shape it and get involved.

Session 14

In the following session's excerpt, the trainers are again active, this time discussing with Mary her behaviour in the group.

Mary. I was just saying that now isn't the time to talk about it.
John (trainer). Now isn't the time, or if I go on with it, I may still not get it across and then that's even worse.
Mary. There again, you are putting ...
John (trainer). Yes, now I am putting words into your mouth.
Mary. ... Value judgements on it — good, bad, worse ...
John (trainer). But Mary, these words, 'right', 'appropriate', I have heard you use a number of times, which raises a question in my mind; to what extent do you anticipate somebody else's response to what you are going to say before you say it? Does that anticipation in many instances prevent you from saying what's inside? Its net effect could be to prevent you from saying as much as you could say.
Mary. It varies very much with where I am and the people I am with. Here, yes, perhaps at the moment, and it need not last, in fact I should be surprised if it did last, because it is not natural except when I feel a certain constraint in a situation.
Jim (trainer). You don't really feel completely safe here yet.
Mary. No, but I feel a lot safer.
John (trainer). Pretty safe, but not safe enough to really let fly (laughter) and take your chances that what you say may be irrelevant or liked or disliked. You are sort of weighing your words and saying, you know, 'I had better say the things that are appropriate and that will win approval' and so forth.
Mary. No, I don't think ...
Jim (trainer). Not necessarily win approval but look appropriate, feel right ...
Mary. Fit.
Jim (trainer). Exactly.
Mary. I don't care about offending anybody. I don't care about anybody saying 'I disagree, ' and I don't care about you all saying, 'We don't like what you are doing. ' It isn't for that reason.

Dick. No, I'd accept that.

Session 16

In session 16, one of the trainers receives some feedback which provides
Ian with an opportunity to try to conceptualise what it is that he has seen
the trainer do in a skilled manner, and which he feels he cannot do.

Ian. It's a very easy focus for those who are not used to thinking in these
sort of terms. I gain the impression that you have been on many T-groups
and not two or three, and you are to some extent practised in looking for
what ought to be obvious to all of us, but only becomes obvious to me when
you put it into words. Therefore, possibly other people find it easier to put
a focus on something, an event which describes the feeling, an event possibly
which is easy to describe here, as that one was, it was very clear, very
simple, and yet it explained Joe's meaning when he gave his principle five
minutes ago.
John (trainer). I am not quite sure what you are saying.
Ian. Well, I personally find it easier to describe an event and say why did
this go wrong, and I get a feedback on what I did and what the other chap did,
rather than, say, ask a question in a vacuum, because even giving an
answer does require practice, because you have to have thought about this
one before you have any idea what you do think. It's like discussing
politics, when you are seventeen, with a few fairly simple ideas and the
whole world is simple, it is either black or it is white. You just learn by
practice that this is not so, and I think this is much the same with this
group in some ways. Some people are naturally good at it anyway, and
some people are not.

Session 17

The next excerpt illustrates several interesting points. At the opening Dick
and Tom are each trying to have their behaviour talked about. This provides
a marked contrast with the early sessions where each member was trying to
direct the attention away from himself. Subsequently, the trainer is
expressing his fears that the effect of the group on Tom is not entirely
beneficial.

Dick. What I want to know now is, do I still come across to you as that kind
of person?
Tom. He has got the discussion off me again!
Andrew (to Dick). If you did, I would tell you. As I said the other day, you
come across entirely differently to me now.
Jim (trainer). Tom, I have been wondering last night and today, whether
there is any possibility that this group intimidated you, that is, I recall you
as saying that you are a spontaneous person and you are a feeling man rather
than a thinking man. The image that I got was that here is a person who

wears his feelings on his sleeve, who is therefore likely to be very
vulnerable. Then I remember the kind of great relief with which you said,
'You know how good it is to have this group, how safe it is,' last Thursday
or Friday.   I am wondering if you really feel that safe?
Tom.   I don't feel intimidated, more stifled. I don't feel at all intimidated.
I can't think of a bunch of chaps less likely to intimidate anybody.
Jim (trainer).   There is something that seems to me, there is something
in the atmosphere or something we have here that makes it difficult for you
to be spontaneous. I get this feeling.

Session 19

A brief episode illustrates more effective giving of feedback. In some of the
earlier excerpts, feedback received from the group was somewhat diffuse and
general. Here it is precise, and linked to a specific behaviour and its
immediate consequences.

Ian.   You give me the impression that the more you mutter 'yes' or
anything to that effect, the faster something is going on behind the 'yes'.
The reverse is that if you don't do it, you are not thinking, but I don't
think that is quite true. I think it makes people wait while you have a quick
think.
Jim (trainer).   And he keeps the floor!
Ian.   I hadn't thought of that, but he does, yes.

Session 20

With the approaching end of the course, group members begin to think of
problems in transferring what they have learned back to their jobs. In this
excerpt the group are discussing the difficulty faced by one of the trainers
who has some information concerning the job settings of several group
members. Although there is a good deal of trust in the group, it is not clear
whether he has the right to pass on information spoken to him earlier in
confidence.

Bill.   This is the important thing isn't it, Joe? You don't see this as a high-
risk situation for John, but John comes across to me very strongly as feeling
it is a high-risk situation for himself. He feels that this is an issue of
confidence, and the feeling that passed a moment or two ago between him and
Alf when he said, 'My God, there I have done it, I have brought this in and I
have put Alf into the position of having to talk about a back-home issue about
which we have private information between us, and I have brought this into
the group and I am responsible for having brought this into the group and I
am feeling I may have put Alf on a spot.' This is a very strong feeling for
you or it was at that moment.
John (trainer).   Yes.
Bill.   You see, this is a high-risk situation because of John's feelings

which cluster round it. You can argue academically that it is a high risk or a low risk, and that is what Joe is doing, but that isn't the important thing at all.

Joe. What I have said is exactly the same as you. I said that this is a high-risk situation for John ...

Bill. Ah yes, OK ...

Session 24

The penultimate session finds the group again considering problems they face in performing effectively on the job. The excerpt gives the beginning of a discussion raised by Joe on difficulties he has in relating to some people he works with.

Joe. One of my problems when I came here, and I am not sure it isn't still, is how to suffer incompetents more graciously. How do we work this one out?

Jim (trainer). How to suffer incompetence — and this is incompetence in other people?

Joe. Well, yes, but not necessarily, but the one or two people I have in mind are not by any stretch of the imagination fools, they are quite highly intelligent people.

John (trainer). Maybe you can do nothing about it, but on the other hand to destroy them only immobilises them completely doesn't it?

Mary. What do you mean by incompetence — that they apparently do not use the talents they have?

Joe. Yes, that's right. In the situation they are in they are incompetent, in any other ten or twelve situations they would be very good.

Mary. Well, one way is to tell them, surely, isn't it?

Joe. Yes, this is what I have done, but I am not sure. This has had a very immobilising effect on them.

Jim (trainer). It seems to me, Joe, that the important thing is to separate acceptance of the person from the rejection of his behaviour.

Session 25

In the final session, the excerpt has a reflective quality as the members look back on the ways their relationships have developed.

Andrew. I didn't realise it to start with, but after a while I realised I had always seen Joe in a boss position, and I thought, what would it feel like to then get around Joe and think of him as a direct subordinate of mine. How would I see him then? What problems would I have on my hands with being the boss man with Joe underneath me, to put it in Joe's terms. This was quite an interesting approach to have towards Joe, I don't know whether anybody else had this sort of feeling because my first reaction to Joe was that he was a boss man with a vengeance. One even feels he is up there and I am down here. A boss atmosphere comes over with Joe on first impact

with him. At least with me it did. So it was nice to try and turn the cards.
<u>Dick.</u> It is a little trick which can sometimes help in getting another view
of people because one can get forged into an attitude towards people.
<u>Joe.</u> I always did a trick like this when I was young. When I listened to
people who talked to me and name dropped, and said you must meet so and
so, he is equal almost to Moses, he is a great writer, and great politician
or great preacher or something like that, I used to feel, as a child, quite
awe-stricken ...

WHAT T-GROUPS ACHIEVE

These excerpts have given some indication of what goes on in the T-group,
we can now return to the question of the goals of the experience. Three
goals were outlined earlier, namely increases in sensitivity, diagnostic
ability and action skill. Since large parts of the latter half of the group's
meetings were given over to sharing impressions of each other's behaviour,
it is clear that each member will have had opportunities to test whether his
expectations about how others saw him are accurate. Similarly, each
member will have shared in discussions of the behaviour and relationships
of others in the group, thereby testing his diagnosis of group behaviour
against those of others. Lastly, each member has been faced with
situations in which he is encouraged to experiment with new behaviours, as
for example in the excerpts from sessions 8 and 17. In each of these two
instances we may wish to ask what happens to the trainee when he goes home.
Will any improvements in these three skills prove to be bounded by the
rather special climate built up within the T-group, or will the improvements
generalise to other situations?

HOW THE T-GROUP ATMOSPHERE IS CREATED

One way to start answering this question is to ask a subsidiary one; what is
it that constitutes the special climate of the T-group? If we can specify this
we may be able to specify also ways in which linkages with situations outside
the training group may be maximised. One essential component of the
T-group is its temporary nature. Miles (1964) has argued that T-groups
have similarities with a wide variety of other temporary experiences, such
as other types of training programmes, holidays, carnivals, therapy, long
journeys, or finite project groups. In all of these settings, to a greater or
lesser extent, participants are protected from the long-term consequences
of their behaviour. In terms of career prospects, long-term obligations or
self-esteem, one simply has less at stake. In these settings participants
tend to behave in less guarded or less cautious ways. They express their
feelings more openly. Early writers on T-groups laid great stress on the
'cultural island' away from organisational pressures as the ideal setting for
the T-group. By isolating the group one makes it much more likely that an

open, trusting climate of relationships will develop, even without specifying anything else about the nature of the experience.

A second major component of the T-group climate derives from the behaviour of the staff member or trainer. T-groups are often described as 'non-directively led' or 'unstructured'. Reference back to the excerpts from the tape, will indicate that this is untrue. The trainer of the T-group typically does indicate his preferences about how the group shall proceed. In this particular group, the trainers did perhaps direct the group somewhat more than the average trainer, but in all groups there is not much doubt that the trainer expresses his preference for having the group talk about their own behaviour.

The third major component of the T-group is the way in which the group is composed. The early writers who saw the T-group as a cultural island stressed that one precondition for the establishment of the 'island' was that the members of the group should be people who did not know one another. A stranger group certainly constitutes more of an island than a group with some continuing relationship. But this is one of the areas in which it is' clear that the early thinking was unnecessarily limiting.

The compositional preconditions for a successful outcome to the T-group are that the members of the group shall provide one another with some support in face of the anxiety which may be provoked by the unfamiliarity of T-group procedure; and that they shall be sufficiently diverse to confront one another with differing views. The amount of confrontation and support found in a stranger T-group will depend on the personalities of those composing the group. If a group is composed of people who work together, the levels of confrontation and support will, of course, in addition be much influenced by the role relationships represented in the group and the climate of relationships in the work organisation.

In a stranger T-group a balance may be arrived at between support and confrontation, but the danger is that there will be more support than confrontation. A highly cohesive group develops but when the trainees return to their jobs they find it difficult to apply their learning in a climate of much lower support. On the other hand, in in-company groups, the danger is that confrontation will outweigh support, which would tend to mean that the T-group members would find it too painful to discuss one another's behaviour. Trainers have developed a variety of methods of building support in in-company training, by prior interventions, tying the training to the working through of specific problems and by modifying the types of intervention made in their groups.

The distinctive components of the T-group climate are that it is a temporary system, which helps the trainer to model an open, trusting style of behaviour. This in turn makes it easier for the group to talk openly to one another, so long as they are composed in such a way as to provide both some confrontation, and some support. The effects of the experience can certainly be eliminated by the trainee's subsequent experiences on the job, but the manner in which the learning is acquired makes it unlikely that this is the normal consequence.

The trainee in the T-group changes because he is influenced by the trainers and the other group members, but the influence is rather unlikely to be compliance or conformity. The influence is much more likely to be based on identification with others in the group or on a process which Kelman (1958) terms internalisation. Internalisation occurs where one accepts influence from another because his values are similar to one's own. I have argued elsewhere (Smith 1969) that the process of internalisation is important in T-groups and is the major determinant of changes which carry over from the T-group to subsequent job performance. The climate of the T-group is precisely the type of setting in which one would expect internalisation to predominate over other modes of influence. If compliance and identification are the most important influence modes in the group, there should be little carry-over to subsequent job performance. If internalisation predominates there should be.

EVALUATING THE EFFECTS OF T-GROUPS

A number of reviews of the evaluation research concerning T-groups have been published in recent years (Campbell and Dunnette 1968; Mangham and Cooper 1969; Smith 1969). The weight of the research evidence is that about two-thirds of the participants in ten-day programmes show changes in subsequent job behaviour which are noticeable six to nine months later. The evaluations have frequently rested on a 'verified change' measure which examines independent descriptions of the trainees' real behaviour and only scores 'real' changes which are verified by two or more describers. The changes found are in the directions implied by the goals of training discussed earlier. Most of these findings apply to stranger groups rather than to in-company training.

There are two principal criticisms of these findings. One is that, although changes have been detected in the trainee's subsequent job behaviour, there is no direct evidence that the trainee is doing his job better as a result. Although true, for some of the evaluation studies, the criticism implies a somewhat naive view of managerial effectiveness. The long-term effectiveness of a manager's performance depends on the interplay of several dozen factors, many of them beyond his control. The nearest we are likely to come to the measurement of effectiveness in the next few years is the use of ratings by work associates of perceived effectiveness. Some of the T-group evaluation studies have used such measures.

At the present time the appropriate strategy is to identify those training needs of managers which can be shown to relate to their perceived effectiveness and design training methods which can satisfy each particular training need. What the research does show is that where the training need is for increase in sensitivity, diagnostic ability and action skill, the stranger T-group can satisfy that need for around two-thirds of the trainees.

The second criticism, which in the UK is associated with the writings of Michael Argyle (1967, 1969; Argyle & Kendon 1967), claims that

T-groups do psychological damage to a significant proportion of trainees.
Argyle even goes so far as to claim that the research studies support his
viewpoint, although the studies he cites do no such thing. No published
follow-up study gives any indication that trainees suffer psychological
damage. It is possible, however, that a small percentage who did not respond
to follow-up researchers might include some who fell in this category. The
information which is required in this area is not so much on whether
psychological breakdowns occur after T-groups, but whether they occur
with any greater frequency than they do in response to the everyday stresses
of organisational life. The difficulty of collecting adequate data on this point
is enormous. For example, some ill-advised firms have selected for
T-group training those managers who they see as neurotic, difficult or
inadequate. This practice has not been widespread and is on the decline, as
firms become better informed about the potentialities of T-group training.
However, it does mean that even if it were shown that more psychological
breakdowns per unit time occurred in T-groups than in the managerial
population as a whole, this might merely reflect unwise trainee selection
rather than anything inherent in the method.

The principal body engaged in T-group training in the USA, National
Training Laboratories, have reported (National Training Laboratories 1969)
that of 14 200 participants in their regular programmes since 1947, 33
(0.2 per cent) have found the experience sufficiently stressful to leave the
programme before the end. The American YMCA have attempted to track
down all instances of 'allegedly severe negative experiences' among 1200
T-group participants. They identified four and, after interviewing them and
their work supervisors, they concluded that in three of the four cases, the
disruptive experience had actually turned out to be beneficial in the long run,
(Batchelder and Hardy 1968). Another point which frequently confuses this
contentious issue in the writings of critics is the use of the term 'breakdown'
to refer to crying. Crying occasionally occurs in T-groups, particularly in
mixed-sex groups. There is nothing inherently harmful in it; indeed it may
be beneficial. It should be distinguished from psychological breakdown,
which is a state requiring medical attention. The emphasis given in this
discussion to the possibility of harmful effects should not be permitted to
overshadow the proven and substantial beneficial effects which researchers
have demonstrated to occur for many trainees.

CURRENT DEVELOPMENTS IN T-GROUP TRAINING

This chapter will conclude with a discussion of the current development of
the T-group method in this country. This has some implications for considering whether a particular programme of training can be relied on to
generate the effects described earlier in this chapter. There are at present
a number of different centres of group training for industry. Those in which
T-groups are most like those described in this chapter are the University
of Leeds and the North London Polytechnic. The trainers at both of

these institutions have been heavily influenced by the tremendous development of T-group methods in the United States. Each institution conducts both stranger T-groups for management and in-company training programmes using the T-group method. As it happens, over half of the contributors to the present volume either are or were in the past employed by one or other of these two organisations.

Another institution with a long history of involvement in group training methods is the Tavistock Institute of Human Relations in London. Tavistock groups are often conducted with a somewhat different emphasis to that so far described. Indeed, they are not typically referred to as T-groups but as 'study groups'. In such a group the staff member's task is to provide a clear and consistent interpretation of what occurs. At no stage in the group is he likely to take up anything approaching a membership role in the group. The interpretations provided are quite likely to be thought out in terms of the descriptive scheme of Bion (1961), although Bion's actual terms would probably not be used in speaking to the group. A full account of the development and rationale for these methods is available in Rice (1965). Under a recent reorganisation, the Tavistock groups are now organised by the Grubb Institute of Behavioural Science. None of the research studies referred to earlier have been concerned with the Tavistock-type groups, thus there is at present no reliable evidence on their outcome.

In addition to these three principal foci of group training, there are considerable numbers of individual trainers in other institutions. They are at present linked by the Group Relations Training Association, a somewhat informal body whose present main purpose is to foster links between those active in the field. Around a dozen British trainers are also Fellows or Associates of EIT (The European Institute for Transnational Studies in Group and Organisational Development). This organisation comprises trainers from a variety of European countries with a particular interest in the application of behavioural science methods to problems arising when organisations cross national boundaries. Their activities in Britain also include the conduct of residential T-group laboratories for senior management and programmes for development of trainers.

Mention should also be made of some of the more formalised adaptations of T-group method to in-company work. Typically an in-company programme would be tailor-made in response to diagnosis of training need, but one or two programmes have acquired a separate identity. The best-known of these is Blake's Managerial Grid. This programme was developed in the United States as a modification of the T-group and has been used substantially by some firms in this country. There are published evaluations of grid programmes (Blake et al., 1964; Smith & Honour, 1969) which suggest that the training does sometimes have marked effects, but not always so. In future, companies will need to devote more attention to whether theirs is the kind of organisation to which grid training is suited.

Another in-company variant is Coverdale training. Here groups are required to organise and perform simple tasks, such as sorting out packs of cards. Group members then evaluate critically their performance and attempt to improve it. It is suggested that this makes training less stressful than the orthodox T-group. There is no published evidence on whether this is so or not, nor any systematic study of the effects of Coverdale training.

The overall picture is one of a steady diversification of group-training methods. This is all to the good in so far as it makes it more likely that training methods appropriate to a variety of settings will be developed. If this promise is to be fulfilled, a continuing flow of evaluation research will be required. Only in this way will it be possible to move from the ebb and flow of prejudice against one method and the fashionability of another to the point where one can logically match training method with training goal in a setting where one knows it will be fruitful.

REFERENCES

Argyle, M (1967) The Psychology of Interpersonal Behaviour
(Harmondsworth, Penguin).
Argyle, M (1969) Social Interaction (London, Methuen).
Argyle, M & Kendon, A (1967) "The experimental analysis of social
performance" in Advances in Experimental Social Psychology,
Volume 3, ed. L Berkowitz (New York, Academic Press).
Batchelder, R L & Hardy, J M (1968) Using Sensitivity Training and the
Laboratory Method : an Organisational Case Study in the Development
of Human Resources (New York, Association Press).
Bion, W R (1961) Experiences in Groups (London, Tavistock Publications).
Blake, R R, et al. (1964) "Breakthrough in Organisation Development",
Harvard Business Review, 42, November-December 1964.
Campbell, J P & Dunnette, M (1968) "The effectiveness of T-group
experiences in managerial training and development",
Psychological Bulletin, 70, 73-104.
Kelman, H C (1958) "Compliance, identification and internalisation",
Journal of Conflict Resolution, 2, 51-60.
Miles, M B (1964) "On temporary systems", in Innovation in Education,
ed M B Miles (Teachers College, Columbia University).
Mangham, I L & Cooper, C L (1969) "The impact of T-groups on
managerial behaviour", Journal of Management Studies, 6, 53-62.
National Training Laboratories (1969) "Emotional stress and Laboratory
training", News and Reports, 3, No. 4.
Rice, A K (1965) Learning for Leadership (London, Tavistock
Publications).
Smith, P B (1969) Improving Skills in Working with People : the T-group
(Department of Employment and Productivity Training Information
Paper 4) (London, HMSO).
Smith, P B & Honour, T F (1969) "The impact of phase I managerial grid
training", Journal of Management Studies, 6.

2

Course designs and methods within the organisation

by Harold Bridger

The distinguishing features of courses, conferences, seminars, projects, study groups and other forms of learning experience have now become less meaningful than before. In practice each type of experience is designed to include aspects of the others, for example through various exercises.

Training experiences for individuals and groups can be said to be an implicit element, to a greater or lesser degree, in all activities occurring in an organisation. It is this on-the-job component of training that provides the greatest headache in establishing criteria for systematic assessment by the Industrial Training Boards : it can range from a sitting-with-Nellie approach (which can be useful or wasteful depending on circumstances) to the essential and selective building of functional skills required in different specialisms. Such learning experiences must be regarded as coming within the terms of reference of internal training even when there are no specific staff designated as teachers. There is, however, a fundamental distinction between experience which contributes to individual or group learning through what is rubbed-off, picked up, or induced through habit-forming, and another kind of learning experience in which the situation itself is explicitly explored and reviewed with the conscious intention of developing people in their roles and contributing to personal maturation in their careers inside or outside the organisation. The later sections of this chapter will define and elaborate this distinction through an examination of the assumptions behind each experience and the accompanying activities.

ORGANISATIONAL SELF-REVIEW AND DEVELOPMENT

A good example of more effective learning from experience is an operational
activity conducted with 'suspended business' sessions to help diagnose and
explore team, committee and other group processes better. The goals of
these sessions are to develop more effective decision-making, leadership,
commitment, interpersonal and role relationships and, not least, more
appropriate active response to current and informed future environmental
changes of many kinds.

In more recent times this internal self-reviewing process and the
implementation of the learning derived from it has come to be known as
'organisation development'. Unfortunately, like so many of the brand
names and jargon terms associated with training techniques and consultancy
packages it has already suffered much debasement in becoming part of the
trail of bandwagons with their specific practitioners and adherents.

Getting an outsider to diagnose and restructure an organisation through a
report may achieve some immediate solutions. However, the price to be
paid (and it may sometimes be necessary) includes the loss of a learning
experience for the organisation's own directors, managers and other
personnel whose day-to-day work and capacity to meet future changes
would have benefited had they performed the diagnosis and restructuring
themselves. What needs to be underlined is that organisational self-review
and development has always been a managerial responsibility even when
the thinking behind it was largely intuitive, when it was expected to go along
with authority and when it was largely concentrated on technological,
economic and competitive conditions and changes.

Taking time out to think through organisational objectives, structural
options and conflicting role relationships with colleagues and/or with
relevant superiors and subordinates is on the increase but still not very
common. The learning experience is still regarded as something of a
luxury, to be engaged in when opportunity permits and to be undertaken in
the hope of a solution or to be sacrificed as part of a cost-reduction
retrenchment exercise (depending on the type of crisis). Looking towards
the near future. however, there is little doubt that the capability of
executives and functional managers to initiate and maintain such processes
with their units and each other will be regarded as an inherent part of the
managerial role itself.

RESPONDING TO A CHANGING ENVIRONMENT

One consequence of the accelerating rate of technological, social, economic,
educational and political changes, acting as forces both from within and
without, is that the enterprise has had to become more capable of
recognising, learning about and responding adaptively to these changes and
forces. Organisationally the enterprise is having to learn how to behave
more as a living organism and to relinquish the tendency to react to events

simply, in mechanistic ways. This entails an organisational change and learning process which affects the way in which the structure of the enterprise and its operational activities are formed and carried out. Patterns of hierarchy, authority and power also have to adapt to increased openness and sharing in decision-making, both in task organisation and in the social development of the enterprise itself. To survive in the next ten years and beyond it will be imperative for organisations of all kinds, local or international, to become more of an open system, that is to be more interactive with and adaptive to their various environments.* It will be necessary to humanise their working activities at all levels or to automate them out.

It will not be enough to make the right return on capital employed, to have the right cash flow figures (where these still continue to be relevant), nor will it be enough simply to think of participation as a good thing or to promote democracy at work as a desirable aim in itself. Development of 'shared responsibility' at work is becoming the crucial issue and is as big a problem for unions and work forces at all levels as it is for industrial managements and policy-making boards. Investing in creativity, whether in the form of innovation or of developing underutilised human resource and talent, has never been easy to balance and optimise against other organisational considerations or boundary conditions such as size, structure, financial resources, and market and political forces acting as pressures internally as well as in the external world.

The implications for people operating at all levels and functions of an open-system organisation (Bridger, 1971) are: increasing 'complexity', 'uncertainty' and 'interdependence'. These dimensions make it necessary to introduce new components into managerial, functional and operating members' roles within organisational life. Under modern conditions, managers are likely to have professional and functional accountability and thereby need to live with and operate within multi-accountability situations. At the same time managers have to accept the imposition of being the leader of a group where people responsible to them in a line situation are likely to have accountability to people who are the leader's colleagues or superiors. In this sense those responsible to us, or as we used to say

---

* An organisation is an open system to the extent to which it is in interaction with its environment and regulates its activities to changing environmental conditions. A closed system regards 'the organisation as sufficiently independent to allow most of its problems to be analysed with reference to its internal structure and without reference to its external environment' (Emery and Trist 1969b, page 281). It implies a rigid boundary between the organisation and its environment or between different functions or departments within the organisation. That is, changes in the environment are not responded to by the organisation; changes in one department are not responded to by another department. To the extent that an organisation is reliant on the environment and its inputs are not constant an open-system approach is more efficient. (Eds.)

'in our group', are not entirely within a closed system. The need to respond to the demands and links external to one's own sphere of influence, both inside and outside the enterprise is referred to as 'boundary condition management'.

How should we train and enable people to anticipate and meet this shift of organisational demands? Before trying to answer this all-important question we should consider forms of learning experience.

TRAINING IN AN 'OPEN-SYSTEM' ORGANISATION

The increasing rates of change in different aspects of the environment together with its consequent complexity and turbulence (see Emery and Trist, 1969a) creates corresponding difficulties for the enterprise. This is especially so in regulating its various forms of exchange with the various parts of that environment which it may wish to influence or work with. For example, technical change and educational development of consumers can affect a market in such a way as to demand internal changes of product, product and process development, technical skills of selling, costing and pricing measures and so on. The objectives and tasks of the enterprise, at any level thus become more and more concerned with the endeavours required to control the boundary conditions of enterprise and environment. Expertise in that environment is consulted more frequently and over an increasing range of issues. In addition, or alternatively, such expertise is brought in or grown internally to ensure the viability and growth of the enterprise.

Forms of organisation and ways of managing are also, in turn, required to adapt to meet the increasing 'openness' of the organisation and the corresponding growing demand for coping with the dimensions already referred to, the complexity and interdependence of people's roles and functions. Uncertainty is already an important element at the boundary of the open-system enterprise but it is intensified and reinforced when the other dimensions are not coped with and developed. Frequently the tendency is to react against uncertainty with defensive measures or on the basis of comforting assumptions about the present or future. What is needed, although it may be painful, are thought, planning and action on the basis of a considered appreciation of what gives rise to the uncertainty. In a recent communication Michel Crozier referred to the power which those who control areas of uncertainty, inside or outside the enterprise, can exercise. Training in various forms can play a central role in controlling uncertainty where it is used 'pro-actively' (a term invented by Charles Handy, Director of Sloan School of Management Studies, London Business School), that is, as part of positive organisational planned action and not 're-actively'. The role, status and calibre of the training function in an enterprise is often a useful pointer to the part it plays in coping with uncertainty in organisational life.

People and units in their efforts to know where they stand personally and

and in terms of their role identity try to clarify, and often over-simplify, their objectives, tighten or firm-up their boundaries and reduce interdependence. Verbally and intellectually people demonstrate that they 'understand' the need to change in order to achieve greater effectiveness. In practice they find themselves in a double-blind, working on unquestioned assumptions, values or standards. What can so often fail to be realised is that we are likely to use the closed-system way of thinking by which our own discipline, profession or management was learned, for dealing with open-system enterprise. We are likely to use our own traditional organisational approach to deal with the objectives concerned with the boundary between the organisation and its environment.

Training is frequently one of those ready panaceas which are latched on to at times of crisis. When we say that 'we never stop learning', fervently adding that 'we are always ready to learn', we mean it but there is the much harder task of unlearning. Unlearning is the phase in the change process which is all too often referred to as 'resistance to change', or more euphemistically as 'human nature' or 'common sense'. At most times we would prefer to proceed to relearning without wanting to face the less comfortable experience of finding out what lies beneath the confusion, conflicts or contradictions. For example, one hears, 'Now we know what's wrong : let's get on with it and not waste time contemplating our navels.' Hence new techniques, revised costing, perhaps new sales training are introduced as the way of 'getting on with it'. The cost of this approach has two components:

1   The obvious cost of developing new skills and other imported or planned changes (this implies that the training role is more likely to be the ancillary service one, that is, not so far away from the concept of trouble shooting)

2   The less obvious cost of contributing little or no real development of people or their roles, either to meet the next boundary-condition control problem, or for their own maturation so as to guarantee them against being deskilled (or without a role) some time ahead. There is little difference in this respect between the shop floor and unions and the more senior ranks of management : one either hears 'time enough when we get a quiet spell and things are not so busy' or 'it's not likely to happen in our neck of the woods, and if it is there are ways of holding it up.'

USES OF VARIOUS GROUP-TRAINING TECHNIQUES

Where cross-functional and multidisciplinary working is treated as a serious and far from simple experience and not just a matter of getting the right mix and assuming the individuals will make things happen through good sense (although this is important in its own right), the gaining of interdependence and the functional leadership appropriate to it, will be of a different order. It is for this reason that the study of groups at work (not just interpersonal relations) and the study of processes of decision-making and behaviour in task-oriented groups, by being in them as a training experience, can be so rewarding. While package courses have their specific uses they do not state their limitations in organisational learning and unlearning terms. For example, learning about 'management style' will not cope with open-system boundary conditions and improved thinking processes cannot resolve conflicting value systems on their own.

Job enrichment, and groups operating on their own 'whole-task' approach as in work-structuring methods, can also be seen as organisational training appropriate to boundary condition management. The preparation of people for such ways of working in an organisation, and particularly preparation at higher levels in the business, is one of the most difficult training tasks today. It is what everyone says he would like but finds difficult to put into practice. The reasons are not far to seek; there is no explicit expectation by the organisation, the manager himself, or even the people in his team that, while the appointed leader could be accountable for the achievement of goals, the unit as a group would need to have shared responsibility for fulfilling and operating the unit tasks. This may sound the same as saying that any one member of the team is responsible for his personal role responsibilities and objectives and for giving his superior his full loyalty as regards the wider unit goals. But it is not the same; in this latter pattern of work organisation the share of responsibility in the unit goals is seen as existing primarily in the superior-subordinate relationship. Nor would this pattern change simply by training the appointed leader to operate with a 'participative style of management'. The basic organisational philosophy, value system and set of expectations can be changed only through an intellectual comprehension of the verbal differences between these concepts. It is for this reason that disappointment frequently follows initial apparently successful and enlightened package-training.

ROLE OF THE 'APPOINTED LEADER'

Learning to adapt to interdependent and shared responsibility for group goals does not entail the elimination of appointed leader roles. There must still be externally directed accountability to the unit's environment, that is to a superior authority, a central administration or another function or institution. The leader is accountable to different aspects of the environment for different things and often to a corporate executive as well.

Internally the appointed leader function will be a climate-setting one. This can be expressed as follows :

1   Leadership is developed through methods of working whereby those holding accountability for specific functions (such as allocation of work, reviewing quality of performance) also learn how to manage

the relevant environmental and boundary conditions so that the group can fulfil its tasks.

2 Decision-making and whole-task management are performed by the group immediately concerned at the appropriate level where such decisions should be made and objectives should be managed, and where, because they 'own' the power and resources, the deployment of human resources can also be most effectively made.

It is training for this form of management — for creating the climate externally and internally, or rather actively balancing and optimising the internal and external environments — for which there is so much need. Managers who have been brought up to think of, and to exercise leadership on the basis of strong internal control and accountability as vested in a single person do not find it easy to unlearn this approach and then relearn their management function as an 'enabling' one. All too often the change is seen as relinquishing power and authority and handing it over to untried people and endangering the achievement of the unit, division or company tasks and objectives. It is also seen as giving up all the skills and values gained in years of experience and venturing into areas of other people's authority oneself, and thereby creating conflictive relations with colleagues. Figure 2:1 shows a comparison of open and closed systems.

ROLE OF TOP MANAGEMENT

Frequently, organisational characteristics play a vital part in allowing one to assess how difficult the training or the unlearning/relearning process is going to be. It is not simply a function of the personality, experience and system of values of resisting managers. An enterprise which structures itself along technical and functional lines so that even quite senior managers reluctantly recognise that the profit centre or whole-task decision-making function is well above their level, creates a climate and condition in which it is very difficult for a manager to change his pattern of working. Even when top management demonstrate by their 'style' that they would welcome more of an open-system approach, the reward-and-penalty system in the organisation is likely to nullify their attempts. For example, heads of very large plants, who operate to given procedures of pricing, cost and market demand, at the same time expect the organisational structure to look after uncertainty and the interdependence and complexity of roles and functions. However true and possible this may have been in the past it will indeed be a rarity in the future.

It is in circumstances such as these that the training manager finds that he is fighting the system and the implicit organisational philosophy when he is simultaneously attempting to fulfil his assigned task and meet the conflicting but equally explicit personnel policy encouraging participative management and cooperation between different functional managers.

The importance of external training opportunities for top management

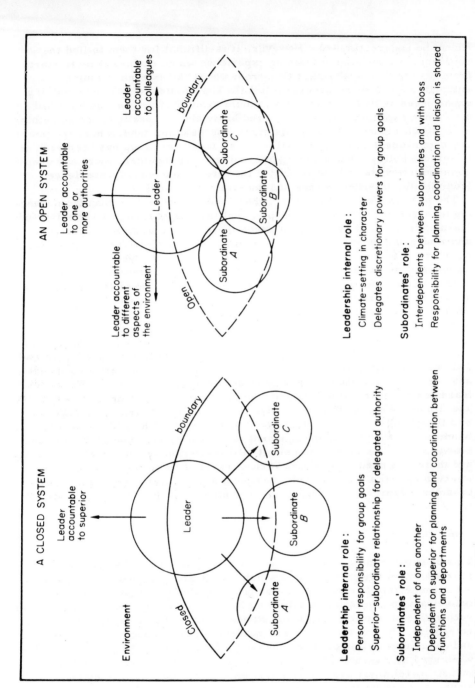

A CLOSED SYSTEM

Environment

Leader
accountable
to superior

Leader

boundary

Closed

Subordinate A

Subordinate B

Subordinate C

Leadership internal role :
Personal responsibility for group goals
Superior–subordinate relationship for delegated authority

Subordinates' role :
Independent of one another
Dependent on superior for planning and coordination between functions and departments

AN OPEN SYSTEM

Leader accountable
to colleagues

boundary

Leader accountable
to one or
more authorities

Leader

Leader accountable
to different
aspects of
the environment

Open

Subordinate A

Subordinate B

Subordinate C

Leadership internal role :
Climate-setting in character
Delegates discretionary powers for group goals

Subordinates' role :
Interdependents between subordinates and with boss
Responsibility for planning, coordination and liaison is shared

Figure 2:1   Some differences between closed and open systems

41

cannot be underestimated. However, it is difficult for them to find the conditions for the kind of training experience which enables them to start from 'where they are' rather than from where the external training authority or school exhorts them to be. The problem of external training experiences is that they need a minimum number of people who have had a common experience to produce credibility and a capacity to 'do something about it' on return to the organisation. On the other hand, where the power and commitment of an individual or small top-level group has been such as to agree a policy for developing internal training together, there are deep common interests and the reality of the three-dimensional experience (complexity, interdependence and uncertainty) to work on.

The principle of starting from 'where people are' rather than from where top management, or training people, feel they ought to be, is not only good learning theory and practice but essential in change processes involving unlearning and relearning. It is essential in adapting to open-system and boundary-condition organisation and is relevant to all levels and functions. Unfortunately it is seldom applied to the design of courses and corresponding events, either inside or outside the enterprise. All too often our learning at school, university, professions and occupations has been built on handed-on knowledge, scholarship and skills rather than through a process of rediscovery and working from known to unknown. There is indeed a corresponding danger in the present day in that we have a large number of information systems and greatly increased opportunities for getting around and arriving anywhere to see places and people. The danger is we do not acquire the 'experience of the experience' simply by arriving. We do not learn how to learn, to innovate and be creative by acquiring more and more knowledge. We need to test reality, to invent our own trials, to risk our own thoughts, values and integrity. And this is why the climate-setting function of authority and management is so important. The boundary conditions need to be such as to permit reality-testing by individuals and groups and there is a need to establish various kinds of 'temporary system' or intervening tasks which permit trying-out and exploration without the all-or-nothing approach to change. This is elaborated in the following section.

THE 'INVISIBLE MANAGEMENT COLLEGE'

This unusual heading refers to the important part played by tasks and courses within the enterprise to which people are assigned not only for some immediate operational aim or goal but where that goal, and the individuals collaborating in achieving it, can be used for building a common recognition of implicit values and standards in the 'culture' of the enterprise. Nor is this merely of academic interest because the existence and awareness of this culture, however informal, can be of practical value when used in enterprise tasks such as selection and training policies, industrial relations problems, management development and appraisal systems and certainly in functional and cross-functional aspects of enterprise life.

Many myths and assumptions grow in an enterprise whereby 'We in X' tend to compare ourselves with other organisations and to think of our- selves and to be treated by the 'centre' or the 'board' in a particular way. It is well that members of a company, regardless of level and function, can often take certain ways of looking at things or of doing things for granted. It has great advantages and equally certain disadvantages in various situations but the values and standards involved need to be examined and judgements made as to their relevance to the enterprise's viability and objectives, or to their effect on operations and practices.

Within the enterprise each different function such as marketing, production, finance, personnel and industrial engineering, has its cultural form. Certainly too the different specialisms have languages of their own quite apart from any jargon or technical communication between in-group members. It is commonplace today to find that people from different countries can develop close personal and role-relationships much more rapidly within a function or discipline (despite certain language barriers) than they can with colleagues of other functions within the same country or even company.

Without setting up any separate specially designed courses or exercises for the purpose it is possible to provide opportunities within current internal courses to study management practices and development. This is so whether the course is purely related to techniques and functions or to wider aspects of multidisciplinary working. What is required, however, is both sanction for training staff members and the training of trainers to work with course members to explore the values and norms of the course or seminar itself. To be of value, the exploration of the way the course has developed and operates as an organisation, including its objectives, management and operational methods, must take place some time before the end of the course to provide a chance for members and staff to review their organisation and see how it might be improved to achieve its objectives better. Thus the training situation becomes an open-system unit in the wider organisation of which it is part, and able to deal with its boundary conditions more effectively.

It is of use to build this study of the course itself into the main course only if there is sufficient time and willingness on the part of the staff or members to allow for the 'institution' to grow values, customs, conventions and so on. It is surprising nevertheless that it takes such a short time to begin recognising the facets of organisational life — the work system, the political system and so on. So that while one does not continually pull up a plant by the roots to assess how it is getting on, every kind of internal course could provide the kind of study that would give a member an increased perception and awareness and even some skill which he might try out with his own people after resuming his role in the enterprise.

As in the organisational self-review and development discussed at the beginning of this chapter the endeavour is to see how far the usually 'invisible' aspects of course life (except in more casual conversations at the bar) can be used constructively for personal development and understanding organisational processes and sub-cultures. There are other ways of designing such experiences without directly exploring the dynamics of the event itself. In one large worldwide organisation, a management selection scheme has been in continuous operation for the past twenty-five years which uses group methods as a central feature of mutual appraisal by selectors and candidates. The selection board sits for one and a half days. During the second day, selectors explore — over a number of events — their changing and cumulative views as individuals, and their shared and compared assumptions, impressions, inferences and opinions with each other, and then again, in interview, with the candidates. Values and standards, whether functional, organisational or by reason of background and experience are discussed in the light of the work of the selection board. Although these values and norms are not explored in the way they would be at a course, there is a recognition that over the years an 'invisible' senior managers' course has been in being for those who have been included on the panel of selectors. More generally it could be said that the learning institution is in session whenever one of the major implicit tasks of a group, actively engaged in doing a job for the enterprise (whether combined with a course or not, and at any level), is that of exploring and agreeing values and standards.

DESIGNING AN INTERNAL COURSE

Rather than begin with concepts, principles and books on management, course designers should use the approach of moving from where members are and establishing the staff and members' base in joint technical or management experience and problems. This involves clarifying for, and with, one another what is agreed as the purpose of the course. Wider generalisations of experience will come later. Principles and practice will be devised which will indicate how the field of work of immediate concern to members can be treated in organisational and management terms. In this way course members will <u>not</u> be faced with trying to find out how any specific form of practice can be 'fitted' to their roles in industrial, professional and other organisations. Part of a pre-course phase would therefore need to be devoted to exploring what members mean by 'the organisation in which we manage or operate our roles'.

The organisation today is, after all, itself the important instrument which is forged to fulfil the mission and objectives of the organisation itself. These in turn lead to setting up tasks and activities; to structuring the organisation by which people fill roles. How far is the organisation seen to be changing shape today to better fulfil the changing means (tasks) by which the objectives (which themselves may undergo change!) can be achieved? This applies as much to the course itself as it does to the wider enterprise. It is therefore part of the design to use the course — and the staff and members' parts in it — as a learning instrument.

Pre-course phase

The pre-course event can either be convened for a set time (say a half or full day) in advance of the course proper or be developed through correspondence combined with some interviewing if not too time-consuming. The purpose of this phase is to:

1 Build a pattern of management interest and needs round which the design of the course can be created to satisfy operational requirements of members and, together with 2 below, to provide a framework introducing some theory and practice gained from other fields in which managers work
2 Build together a pattern of problems based on personal experience and practice which can be shared and studied with others in the course

Course phase

Work in many centres in Europe and the United States over the last twenty years has developed group methods which permit members to study job problems in their own work and to share and compare them with other members. These methods include innovative exercises, case studies and business games. The experience of designing, developing and studying the groups' own learning can be brought into the exploration, and so can some theoretical and empirical findings in the behavioural sciences. By bringing these separate aspects together in a systematic and concentrated way the chances of experimental learning are increased; learning 'how' rather than learning 'that'.

The use of 'study groups'* provides an opportunity for members to share their experiences and to compare problems and situations. A staff consultant might attempt where relevant to indicate certain features of the process operating in the group. At other times group work can be suspended to explore methods of working which the group has evolved. Other smaller groups (trios and quartets) can focus on specific cases and incidents prepared by members from their own working experience and practice consulting, counselling and giving and taking advice. Large groups or plenary meetings may have several functions, including studying relevant concepts and research findings, and communication exercises.

Intergroup communication and organisational review and development can be studied through using the course itself and the roles of members and staff in its operation, not only as a learning instrument but as a way of incorporating new ideas and needs.

---

*Study group is here used in an internal course context; the group's discussion is centred around the concerns of the organisation and the management of it as well as the study of the group's own process or dynamics. Elsewhere in the book 'study group' refers to an external course held by the Tavistock Institute (editors).

The last phase of the course itself would include an 'interim evaluation' to concern itself with:

1   Criticisms of the course and how it might be improved;
2   Planning and setting tasks for the post-course phase in the back-home setting;
3   Setting another date by which to relate back to each other and explore how far learning has been applicable and what successes or difficulties were encountered

EVALUATION OF COURSES

Whether the objective of a particular course is training for special skills, general management training, functional development or learning about group and organisational processes there are certain common criteria which need to be fulfilled.

1   To what extent have course members 'contributed' to the decision to attend? Do they feel they have been 'sent' for one purpose or another; for example, to correct deficiencies, for development or for potential promotion? Expectation and preparation are of great importance and the underlying message attached to attending internal courses is apt to reflect the political, status and reward systems within the organisation.

2   One crucial element of a course is the opportunity it provides for trying oneself out in situations which are not the crunch issues which occur in the reality of operational life. If this testing-out opportunity is accompanied by some form of reporting back to local authority in the member's own unit, the testing-out is likely to be very restricted or a form of acting-the-part. (As one barman in a pub was heard to remark — 'It always seems to me that the real course is taking place here, away from the staff.') The degree of confidentiality on performance is another pointer to the system of training values.

3   A further feature of a similar order is the need of course members to feel that they can use knowledge and experience which they have brought to the course. Apart from any contribution which they might make individually or jointly there is the opportunity, which is missed in most internal courses, for obtaining the constructive and innovative ideas of members on wider enterprise problems and issues. Increasingly there are a greater number of projects or operational considerations included in courses as relevant features for application purposes. Equally, more opportunity is being given for members to bring and work out problems with others, including staff, while on the course. Where possible, members should be

encouraged to study certain relevant issues with colleagues in their own unit as part of the pre-course phase. This not only provides a basis for learning and trying-out during the course but provides a basis for re-entry and communicating course ideas to colleagues on return.

4   There will always be a degree of self-appraisal in addition to any performance appraisal which may have been carried out by the nominating manager. The opportunity for tutoring and/or counselling members while on a course in group or individual form is seldom taken usually, it is said, because there is 'not enough staff time.' The underlying reason, however, is because the course is oriented towards handing over knowledge and information rather than allowing members 'to learn how to learn'.

Apart from these general points it will be realised that evaluation of training and learning cannot be dealt with by a 'before and after' assessment or judgement. Certain instructional and written-examination-type courses can be treated in this way and provide a sort of qualification for the course members. In courses where the objectives are multi-purpose, and where the design and methods attempt to develop the course members personally as well as functionally or managerially, evaluation of the course will be much more complex. Not only is there the long-term learning effect as against the short-term but either can be jeopardised or supported by the enabling climate, or lack of it, in the unit from which the member comes. Although all evaluations can be regarded as 'interim'. such an event should not just be carried out at the end of any course but at the mid-way or two-thirds point in the course where it can be used for reviewing the 'where we are' and exploring what changes might be made in the rest of the course bearing in mind the total experience so far. The concluding 'where do we go from here' can then be so much more productive, for the enterprise as well as for the individual.

REFERENCES

Bridger, H (1971) Discussion note in Teamwork for World Health
(CIBA Foundation Blueprint) ed. G Wolstenholme & M O'Connor
(London, J & A Churchill), pages 186-90.

Bridger, H & Wilson, A T M (1946) 'Group discussion,' British
Council Review.

Emery, F E & Trist, E (1969a) 'Causal texture of organizational
environments,' in Systems Thinking ed. F E Emery
(Harmondsworth, Penguin), pages 241-57.

Emery, F E & Trist, E (1969b) 'Socio-technical systems,' in
Systems Thinking ed. F E Emery (Harmondsworth, Penguin),
pages 281-96.

3

Managerial Grid training: an application in ICI Pharmaceuticals Division

by George Clark

In this chapter the basic concepts of Blake and Mouton's Managerial Grid will be outlined and a practical application of it at the Macclesfield Works of ICI Pharmaceuticals Division will be described.

The Managerial Grid of Blake and Mouton is a concept upon which is built a systems approach to organisation development divided into two major parts. The first is concerned essentially with communications and interaction between individuals and groups of individuals. An input of theory and some experimentation within groups of people in a low-risk training situation is followed by developing the natural work groups. Subsequently, problems between groups are tackled so that a problem-solving culture is evolved to deal with problems of both an intra- and inter-group nature. The second part of Blake and Mouton's total approach is to produce and implement a corporate strategic model (that is, a total business strategy for the organisation) so that the organisation can reach its objectives in an effective way.

The major difference between Blake and Mouton's method and that of many other group-training activities is that Blake and Mouton regard the organisation as the primary target and not the individual or isolated groups of individuals. Groups of people can be brought together who have the same training needs — for example, to develop leadership skills, to improve decision-making or problem-solving skills — but such group activities might be classed under management development rather than organisation development. To make the difference clear, management development aims at increasing the knowledge and developing the skills of managers so that they may contribute more to the organisation whereas organisation development seeks to create the environment in which the managers can make this contribution in an effective way.

Another important characteristic of the Managerial Grid is the highly structured approach. Participants work through a number of activities which are very directive but which when followed closely provide the necessary learning experience. The advantage is that relatively in-experienced instructors can be used for in-company training purposes. (The term 'relatively inexperienced instructors' should not be taken as meaning anyone would be acceptable as a trainer — the basic criteria of sensitivity and understanding of the learning process are essential but a trainer as such would not require a further lengthy period of training in the Grid method to be an effective Grid instructor.) A disadvantage is that the training seems to be rigid and inflexible thereby creating some resistance and a feeling that everyone has to go through the same sausage machine.

THE GRID CONCEPT

The Managerial Grid derives its name from the method of representing the principal managerial styles. Blake and Mouton, in common with many other behavioural scientists, see a manager's role as being concerned with two major factors :

1   The work (or tasks) to be undertaken.
2   The people with whom he associates (bosses, peers and the subordinates who are concerned with carrying out the task).

These two factors are not seen in isolation but as interdependent. Blake and Mouton are more specific in considering not so much 'task' and 'people,' but the concern for the task (or production as Blake and Mouton call it) and the concern for people. By representing the concern for production and the concern for people on two axes, Blake and Mouton construct a graph or Grid (see Figure 3:1) which by numbering each axis from 1 to 9 gives convenient coordinates for describing five principal managerial styles. Blake and Mouton then outline the characteristics of each managerial style and how such managers deal with 'production' (which includes not only 'nuts and bolts' production but production of ideas and decisions), conflict and creativity. They also consider the effect of various external conditions upon the way these principal managerial styles may alter. A strong indication is given that (9, 9) is the ideal style which by showing maximum concern for both production and people meets the objectives of both the organisation and the individuals within it.

The above is a highly simplified precis of ideas which are dealt

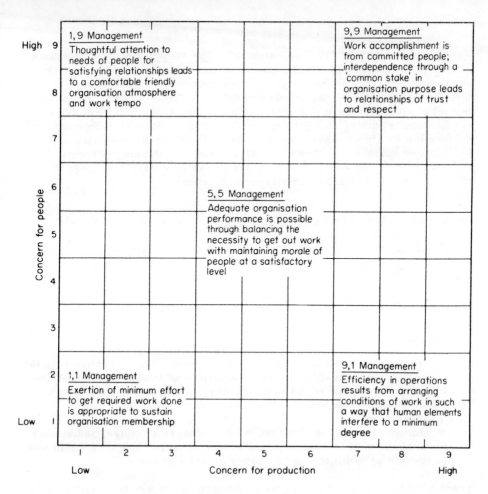

Figure 3:1   The Managerial Grid describing five principal managerial styles
Reproduced from The Managerial Grid by R R Blake and J S Mouton,
by permission of the authors

with at some length in Blake and Mouton's <u>The Managerial Grid</u> (Houston, Texas, Gulf Publishing, 1964). Based on this background theory, Blake and Mouton have derived a six-phase programme for organisation development which they term Grid Organisation Development. A certain amount of confusion arises when speaking of the Managerial Grid as to whether one is talking about the whole Grid Organisation Development programme or simply phase 1 of the Grid. Probably the majority of people when speaking of 'The Managerial Grid' are thinking in terms of phase 1 but it is somewhat unjust to take phase 1 by itself and judge the effectiveness of the Grid on this experience alone.

GRID ORGANISATION DEVELOPMENT

The phases of Grid Organisation Development are as follows:

Phase 1

This is an educational phase with the following objectives:

Personal learning.

1 To learn more about the Grid. This involves learning particularly the five principal Grid styles and the variations to these principal styles.
2 Based on knowledge of the managerial styles, the participants to a phase 1 seminar are then able to learn more about their own managerial styles.
3 In addition to learning about their own managerial styles, individuals learn about their own managerial values; that is, how they would like to operate as distinct from how they actually operate.

Team Action. In a series of group discussions the seminar participants learn:

1 What team effectiveness means.
2 The value of frank and open discussion in improving effectiveness.
3 The value of reviewing how well the team is operating and planning improvement steps.

Interaction between groups. A learning activity is set up which demonstrates in an intergroup situation the counter-productive nature of:

1 Stereotyping individuals and groups of individuals.
2 Conflict which is resolved by producing a winner and a loser.
3 Destructive criticism.
4 The factors which cloud perception.

Organisation culture.

1   The present culture of the organisation is explored, and
2   Ways of learning how to improve the organisation are developed.

Time utilisation.   The whole seminar is planned in a way which shows the need to utilise time effectively.

In order to gain maximum learning from phase 1, it is structured in such a way as to encourage risk taking and experimentation. Thus a team in a phase 1 seminar would contain no boss/subordinate relationships or indeed peer relationships in a family group.

Phase 2

Phase 2 aims at putting into practice the theory and learning gained from phase 1. The learning experience of phase 1 enables the teamwork development in phase 2 to begin in an atmosphere of free and frank discussion and with a knowledge that an effective team can make a significant contribution to reaching the goals of the organisation. Unlike phase 1 it is concerned with the family group of boss and subordinates and it is set up as a business meeting in which the boss operates as he would normally with his group of subordinates.

   There are five activities in phase 2 :

Activity 1   is a team examination of how it operates under the following headings :

1   Teamwork
2   Objectives
3   Planning
4   Communications
5   Traditions, precedents and past practices
6   Critique (looking inward at how the team operates)
7   Initiative
8   Facing up (to problems)
9   Standards of performance
10 Profit

By considering how the team would like to operate and how it actually operates, lists of problems are derived dealing with work items (operational problems), problems affecting how the members operate (intra-group problems) and, arising fortuitously, interpersonal problems and intergroup problems.

Activity 2   is a personal review of how each team member operates and ends with plans for personal improvement opportunities.

<u>Activity 3</u>   is designed to establish improvement goals for the problems identified in Activity 1.

These first three activities form the core of the teamwork development phase.

<u>Activity 4</u>   is concerned with future teamwork development in which the team decides whether or not to continue teamwork development down the line.

<u>Activity 5</u>   is a review of the progress made against the action plans derived in Activities 2 and 3 and takes place some three to six months after the initial teamwork development activity.

A model of phase 2 is shown in Figure 3:2.

<u>Phases 3 to 6</u>

Phases 1 and 2 have been described in some detail since it is by tackling real live problems in the work context that the knowledge and understanding of the Grid concepts gained from phase 1 can be put into practice and a return on the time and money invested obtained.

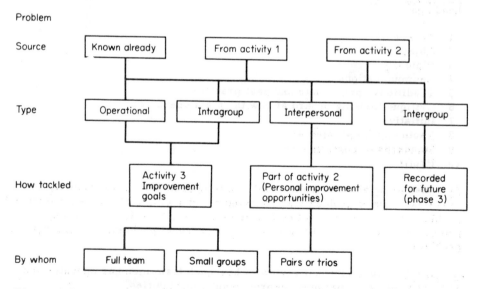

Figure 3:2   Model for phase 2 teamwork development

In less detail the other phases are :

Phase 3   This deals with the problems which arise between groups —
it deals with the intergroup situation. Here again the approach is structured,
in that questions have to be answered which lead to isolation of the problem
and the formulation of action plans between the groups.

Phase 4   is concerned with designing an ideal strategic corporate model,
(that is, a total business strategy for the organisation) and involves the
organisational leaders — usually the board of directors.

Phase 5   Having determined what the business is and where it is going
this phase deals with the implementation of the plan leading to an improvement in the business effectiveness of the firm itself.

Phase 6   is a diagnostic tool to ascertain how the business has improved.
Alternatively phase 6 can precede phase 1 to permit the organisation to
see where the major problems lie.

WHY ICI CHOSE THE MANAGERIAL GRID

In the middle 1960s ICI decided that the rapidity of change in the general
business and social environment demanded a rethinking of the overall
personnel policy. There was a need by the company to increase productivity
and for prices to be as stable as possible, but at the same time it had to
meet the requirements of employees for a steadily increasing standard of
living. There were indications that, in addition to increased remuneration,
the manual workers would appreciate a non-fluctuating weekly salary as
distinct from a wage calculated on a basic hourly rate plus job rating plus
an incentive bonus designed to reflect individual output.
   Most schemes based directly on an output/money basis tend to generate
conflict between management and men which in the long run is against the
best interests of the company. This is because men doing the work are
not motivated to declare to management improved methods of operating or
greater effectiveness achieved due to increased job knowledge, or additional
acquired skills, since the information would lead to a redesign of the job
and a reduction in potential bonus.
   Management are faced with frequent updating of incentive schemes
(rarely achieved) or using financially rewarding suggestion schemes
(only partly successful). Thus, much information and creativity residing
at the shopfloor level is hidden from management when an incentive bonus
scheme is in operation.
   Add to this, on the one hand, organisation and supervisory structures in
need of critical examination and, on the other hand, the demarcations
operated between differing tradesmen and between tradesmen and non-
tradesmen, then it can be seen that there was considerable scope for

improving effectiveness.

It was against such a background that in 1965 the company and the signatory unions entered into a trial agreement designed to have an entirely new look at the method of performing work and the relationships between trades and non trades and between the manual workers and the supervisors. The incentive bonus scheme was to be scrapped and the entire working force graded into eight grades based on an annual salary to be paid weekly. The manual workers would thus cease to be paid by the hour as formerly and become weekly paid staff.

The problem facing management was to implement this agreement in a way which would increase the effectiveness of the manufacturing units; to do this in the absence of an incentive scheme and to tackle the question of demarcations and the method of supervising work. This meant that managers at all levels had to rethink the way they managed and also had to develop a new form of organisation.

As background to the problem facing the Pharmaceuticals Division of ICI, some information on the Division may be of interest. The Division has slightly over 3000 employees of which 1800 are monthly paid staff and 1200 weekly paid staff (ie those now covered by the company-union weekly staff agreement). 35 per cent of the Division staff are women. Of the monthly paid staff, over 500 are graduates of which nearly three-quarters are employed on research.

The two major sites of the Division are the headquarters area housing research, marketing and administration and Macclesfield (seven miles from headquarters) where the principal manufacturing works is sited together with three headquarters departments having close association with the works. 15 per cent of the monthly paid staff on the Macclesfield site are of graduate status, mainly chemists and pharmacists, but with engineers, accountants and graduates who have specialised in various 'staff' functions, such as personnel, management sciences and training. The supervisory group span a wide range of knowledge and experience from the junior supervisor appointed from the ranks of the weekly staff to young graduates gaining production experience.

The first task in tackling the implementation of the company-union agreement and relating it to the Macclesfield site was to devise a strategy in terms of organisation development rather than simply devising a training programme for imparting new knowledge to the management concerned. At Macclesfield, those most directly concerned were some twenty-nine managers and forty-four supervisors in the works and distribution areas. These key people required training by an effective group-training method as part of a change programme in which sound relationships and high interpersonal skills would be seen as an essential part of business effectiveness.

Whilst there were a number of attractive theories available — for example, McGregor's Theory X and Theory Y, Likert's Diagnostic Instrument based on his four system categorisation of management — there were few ready-made systems available as teaching methods. In

1966, the only two systems available as packages were the Reddin Three-Dimensional Grid and Blake and Mouton's Managerial Grid. The Managerial Grid was selected for further examination first because more knowledge in the UK was available about it and second, on examination it appeared to have advantages because it could be run fairly easily on an in-company basis by company instructors after a short training programme.

HOW THE GRID WAS INTRODUCED

Having taken the decision to investigate further the use of the Managerial Grid as the basic training activity for implementing the agreement between the company and the unions (now known as the Weekly Staff Agreement — WSA) the WSA coordinator (a person appointed to advise on all WSA matters across the Division) participated in a phase 1 seminar run by Scientific Methods Inc. (SMI) — the business organisation of Blake and Mouton. This was a successful experience so an approach was made to the management of the Macclesfield site — the major production site of Pharmaceuticals Division.

The target was to help to develop the management from the first-line supervisor to the senior managers on site in order to implement, as effectively as possible, the Weekly Staff Agreement. The first essential was to gain the commitment of the two senior managers on the site who controlled between them almost the whole of the manual workers. These two managers were the Works Manager, in charge of all the manufacturing operations, and the Distribution Manager responsible for the warehousing of the products and their distribution from the works.

In discussion, both managers agreed to attend a phase 1 seminar run by SMI. It was agreed that should the two managers not find the phase 1 seminar a useful experience then the Managerial Grid would not be introduced on the site and some other form of organisation development would be considered. In the event both managers were enthusiastic after attending the seminar and plans were made to continue further with the Managerial Grid. Partly for status reasons and partly to gain time to plan and develop an in-company phase 1 seminar, several of the senior management attended external SMI seminars. From these senior managers a number were selected to be trained as instructors as well as the coordinator, and then in-company seminars were started.

It was considered an important point to have a high proportion of line managers as instructors since the whole activity could then be seen as important to the people directly concerned and not just another training activity. For the first seminar an experienced grid instructor from else-where in the company was available to help Pharmaceuticals Division instructors. The first seminar was run with four teams of six but, with further experience and confidence, later seminars were run with eight teams of eight.

Against the background of managers and supervisors having completed phase 1 of the Grid, further training was undertaken dealing with problems of communication, group discussion leading and problem solving, so that discussions with the manual workers could proceed in an effective manner and new jobs designed in ways which motivated the operatives themselves to be more effective.

PHASE 1 EXPERIENCE

Participant experience

Whilst there is always a variety of responses to any group training, it is fairly easy to predict the reactions of people during the week seminar of phase 1 of the Grid programme. The first reaction tends to be one of hostility to the highly structured form of the phase 1 seminar which is something the trainer has to recognise and for which he has to be fully conversant with the rationale for each activity. There is also strong criticism of the book, The Managerial Grid, by Blake and Mouton which, in British eyes, is a badly written or at least a long-winded textbook to study. Also the methods used in the seminar for scoring and recording progress are seen as somewhat artificial. Nevertheless these criticisms pass and, by the end of the seminar, there is fairly widespread agreement on the value of the training which is seen as a stimulating, helpful experience.

On returning to the job, most participants feel a need to put into practice what they have learned on the seminar. In the early days at Macclesfield those responsible for introducing the Grid training together with the local management were guilty of not taking advantage of this enthusiasm to do further group building in a systematic way. Thus, after some time, differing views were expressed on the value of Grid training largely dependent upon the opportunities or lack of opportunities which had been provided to carry out further group development work. Those who were quickly able to become involved in the WSA discussions were able to utilise knowledge gained on the Grid seminar and generally continued to regard the training as valuable. Others who had less opportunity tended after a while to see the training as of interest, but not directly applicable in their particular jobs.

Trainer experience

In the course of running the seminars a number of experiments were tried regarding the composition of the groups. At one extreme, a group was composed of participants of equal or nearly equal status — for example, all graduates or alternatively all first-line supervisors — and at the other extreme, a group was composed of an entire so-called diagonal slice from a senior graduate in one section to a junior first line supervisor in another section. Whilst status is only one criterion for selecting group members and indeed may be considered an irrelevant one, experience in running phase 1 Grid seminars has suggested that members should not all be of the same status level but that the mix should not be too wide. The term status is used here not only to denote position in the hierarchy but also the different categories of tasks carried out, for example, 'thinking' and 'doing'. By and large the first-line supervisors who were essentially practical men found the discussion of somewhat abstract points more difficult than, for example, the graduates who were more at home in such a situation. Nevertheless very few individuals failed to get there in the end. In trying to arrange groups two differing requirements have to be considered. First, the needs of senior people who are able to grasp a point quickly and want to get on as against the junior person who has to work more slowly and, second, the learning that both senior and junior people gain from each other by an appreciation of their differing problems and methods of thinking and working.

To maintain the enthusiasm gained in the phase 1 seminars and to build a bridge from this educational phase to the work situation, SMI have recently been encouraging the tackling of so-called phase 1A projects.

PHASE 1A PROJECTS

Phase 1A projects are selected from problems which are usually known to the participants but have not been tackled in the past. Criteria for phase 1A projects are :

1   The problem should be short term; it should be possible to 'solve the problem within three months'. The reason for this is that one wants to have the phase 1A projects out of the way before phase 2.
2   The problem should be of an operational nature. This is to say, it should not be an interpersonal or attitudinal problem but one which really concerns the tasks upon which the group is engaged.
3   The problem should 'hurt'. By this it is meant that it is a real live issue which if solved would achieve a real improvement in the organisation's performance.
4   Criteria should be available to judge when the problem has been solved. This is to say that issues like 'improved communications' are not the sort of problems which should be tackled in phase 1A, as there is no end product by which one can say this has been achieved.
5   The problem which is tackled must be one which is supported by the boss and which the boss believes to be an important issue.

Work on phase 1A projects carried out elsewhere has indicated that this approach is a useful link between the phase 1 seminar and the team building carried out under phase 2.

EVALUATION

At Macclesfield, no attempt was made as a separate study to evaluate phase 1 training as such but subsequently, in another location, such a survey was made. In this unit, in which twenty members had done phase 1 some three to four months earlier, a ten-question questionnaire was given. The questionnaire was constructed around declared objectives of the phase 1 seminar. Five questions dealt with issues of understanding (of the various managerial styles; of one's own managerial style; of the value of teamwork; of the factors affecting conflict and of the type of organisation in which the individual would like to work).

Four questions dealt with aspects of phase 1 learning which might reasonably be expected to transfer back to the job (frankness and candour with colleagues; frankness and candour with the boss; frequency of making critiques and ability to organise time at work). The final question dealt with alteration in the participants' own managerial values.

The results of the questions dealing with issues of understanding are summarised on a five-point scale in Figure 3:3.

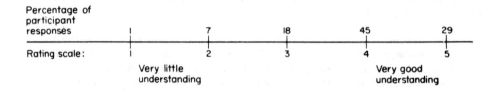

Figure 3:3   Member ratings of understanding gained from a phase 1 seminar

It can be seen from these responses that approximately three-quarters of those attending the seminars had achieved either good or very good understanding of the topics covered in the phase 1 seminar.

The results of the four questions dealing with those aspects of the phase 1 learning which might reasonably be expected to transfer back to the job are summarised in Figure 3:4.

It requires persistence from the individual and support from the environment for learning to be translated from the seminar to the live work situation and the group had been rather less successful in this area than in that of understanding. In particular, the use of critique and the effective utilisation of time left scope for further improvement. On the other hand, both with colleagues and with bosses there was an improvement in frankness and candour. The participants felt that there was little difference in the degree of candour shown whether with their colleagues or

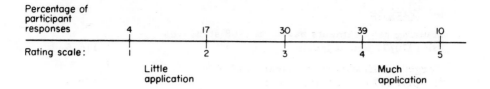

Percentage of participant responses	4		17		30		39		10

Rating scale: 1   2   3   4   5

Little application   Much application

Figure 3:4 Member ratings of application of learning from a phase 1 seminar

with the boss.

The final question dealing with how far the participants' own managerial values had altered showed responses spreading from 'not at all' to 'considerably'.

At the Macclesfield site of ICI

In considering the value of phase 1 training at Macclesfield it has to be appreciated that it was introduced into the Pharmaceuticals Division of ICI as a means of helping to implement the Weekly Staff Agreement (WSA) and that to have set up a control experiment would not have been feasible. Comments on the successes of the Managerial Grid at Macclesfield are therefore partly subjective and partly bound up with the total WSA exercise. Thus the quantitative data given below cannot be attributed solely to the effects of phase 1 Grid, but undoubtedly the Grid played a significant part in achieving the results.

A subjective assessment by those involved indicated that the frankness and openness created by the phase 1 seminar was a significant factor in enabling useful discussions to be carried out in depth with both junior management and the manual workers themselves. In addition, the knowledge of managerial styles and values and greater skills in dealing with conflict undoubtedly had a valuable effect.

The quantitative data given in Figure 3:5 relates to the first year of implementation of the Weekly Staff Agreement at Macclesfield Works. As already stressed it would be incorrect to ascribe all these results to phase 1 of the Grid, but some credit must go to it as the starting point for the whole operation. The manning figures show that an estimate made at the time of implementation of the Weekly Staff Agreement forecast that nearly 7 per cent fewer people would be required overall to meet the production demand. In practice, after the first year of operation, nearly 17 per cent fewer people were required than would have been the case under previous manning schedules. The financial figures show that an estimate made at the time of implementation of the Weekly Staff Agreement indicated a loss

1   Manning (all staff - managers and supervisors as well as operatives)

Reference year 1968 = 100

(a) Targets

Manning requirements based on 1968 standards for 1970/71 output levels	116.5
Target for first year of operation of WSA (1 April 1970 - 31 March 1971)	108.5
Reduction in manning (%)	6.9

(b) Achievement*

Manning requirements based on 1968 standards at 1 April 1971 allowing for 60% increase in output over 1968	129
Achieved - 1 April 1971	112**
Reduction in manning achieved (%)	16.7

*   In a rapidly developing works the production rate is continuously increasing so that targets have to be recalculated to meet this dynamic situation. The figures quoted are those of the 'hard headed' production managers.
**   The reductions achieved were chiefly in management numbers rather than operatives.

2   Financial

Reference year 1968. Calculations below are related to each £100 000 spent in wages and salaries in 1968.

(a) Targets   £

Cost of wages and salaries for manning requirements April 1970/March 1971 on pre-WSA basis adjusted for increased cost of living, normal adjustments, etc.	137 765
Target based on reduced manning at higher WSA rates of pay.	142 490
Anticipated loss	4 725

(b) Achievement £

Cost of salaries for manning at increased output
levels on pre-WSA basis adjusted as above   153 095

Achieved (31 March 1971)   149 460

(c) Indirect savings (improved quality of products,
reduced retreatment of products, improved plant
utilisation)   11 460

3 Other Factors of Achievement

	April 1970 (%)	April 1971 (%)
Overtime (on normal working hours)	8.5	6.5
Sickness absence (annual)	4.3	3.7
Total absence (annual)	6.6	4.5
Accident frequency (on overall attendance hours)	0.03	0.03
Voluntary turnover (related to average numbers employed)	38.6	13.3

Figure 3:5 Macclesfield site : experience after
one year's operation under WSA conditions

of £4700 per £100 000 salary bill due to increases in pay notwithstanding a
reduction in the manning requirements. At the end of the first year of
operation there was a direct saving of £3600 and indirect savings of nearly
£11 500 per £100 000 salary bill. The reduction in overtime working and
the numbers of people leaving the firm voluntarily are significant and
represent a hidden saving to the company against the estimated financial
picture. It is, of course, not possible to say how much these improvements
are due to higher salaries or to more attractive methods of handling the
work tasks.

ALTERNATIVE PROCEDURES

On the debit side and with hindsight, it would have been better to have
planned a total strategy not only for carrying phase 1 down the line but
also to implement phase 2. The carrying out of planned phase 2 team-
building exercises with the consequential development of a problem-solving
culture would probably have given a more substantial base than simply

using phase 1 followed by ad hoc group discussions where there was less attempt at team building. On the other hand, there was considerable pressure on the production people to get down to detailed discussion on how to implement the WSA principles and to have proceeded down the line with formal phase 2 sessions would have been too big a burden to carry.

It would also have been an advantage to have proceeded with phase 1 in vertical slices through the organisation rather than horizontally which, by and large, was the way the Managerial Grid was operated. In other words, to have selected one or two units and to have put everyone through, from the manager to the first-line supervisor, would have enabled these units to have had a similar educational and unfreezing experience in a relatively short time upon which to build subsequent activities.

GUIDELINES FOR USING MANAGERIAL GRID TRAINING

Based on personal experience of introducing Blake and Mouton's Managerial Grid to the Pharmaceuticals Division of ICI, the following guidelines are suggested.

1   The first essential is to appoint a person to be an internal adviser who acts as the focal point for organisation development.

2   An early task of this person is to determine the key people who can influence the system, and to gain their agreement for acting as 'seeds' on an external SMI phase 1 seminar.

3   If this group (which may be no more than two or three) is favourably inclined to a programme of Grid work then it is necessary to check what it is intended to achieve. There must be a commitment to developing the organisation (which may be a discrete part of the total) and not simply to seeing the Managerial Grid as part of management development. A view which is heard from time to time is that it would be useful to send certain individuals on the Grid 'to do them good'. This is not a sound reason for introducing Managerial Grid training.

4   If there is a commitment to introduce the Managerial Grid, then it is necessary to plan a strategy to include at least both phase 1 and phase 2 of the Managerial Grid. Phase 1, carried out off site and in a risk-free situation, is a valuable experience, but the payoff comes when the family groups are able to do some team building and problem solving as a group (phase 2).

5   If the numbers involved in the organisation warrant running in-company seminars then some of the participants who have already done a phase 1 seminar should be selected for instructor development. Initially the training should be done with SMI but later in-company training is possible.

6   In planning in-company seminars, briefing before sending people on a phase 1 will pay dividends. The appropriate line manager should interview each person to explain the background to organisation development and where the individual fits in. This session is also important to judge the reaction of the individual. A successful outcome would be a commitment on the part of the person to attend the seminar; a minimum requirement is to have a sceptical volunteer. A person who does not wish to attend should not be coerced into so doing. Trainers may be used to explain the mechanics, deal with queries and emphasise essential requirements, such as the need for completing fully the prework, countering some of the horrific stories of previous participants, and dealing with the problem of stress.

7   As with other types of group training, certain individuals find the phase 1 seminar somewhat taxing, particularly since the work is challenging and tends to involve lengthy group discussions. Although not encouraged by the trainers, groups tend to work late — not infrequently into the early hours of the morning in the open-ended activities — which may also upset the normal routine of participants. As a precaution it is advisable to dissuade an individual from attending a phase 1 seminar if he is known to be under mental stress or physically off colour at the time.

8   The internal adviser should keep a check on the agreed programme, not only for the phase 1 seminars, but for arranging the phase 2 programme (for which he should also be trained as a consultant) and ensuring that line managers are helped in following up each case. It has been found useful to follow up a phase 1 seminar (or preferably starting the process on the last day of the seminar) by agreeing some phase 1A projects. Apart from the motivation, which success brings in phase 1A projects, it also develops a commitment to tackling deeper problems in a phase 2 session and starts the development of a problem-solving attitude.

PART TWO

TRAINING
ON-GOING WORK GROUPS

4

Building an effective work team

by Iain Mangham

One of the classic problems of sensitivity training is what happens to the
individual when he returns to his organisation. As Pugh (1965) puts it :
'When he returns to his job, the organisational demands are the same and
so are the expectations of the other members in their roles, with whom
he has social relationships.' Individual effectiveness is only partially a
function of a person's insights and awareness. Real work effectiveness is
also enhanced or inhibited by the person's immediate working environment.
The reviews of current research by Mangham and Cooper (1969) and
Campbell and Dunnette (1968) came to similar conclusions in so far as they
noted evidence of individual change, but no hard evidence to support the
often expressed hope that sensitivity training facilitates organisation
change. What evidence there is (Friedlander 1966, 1968) is based upon
'training the system' rather than training the individuals.

The second classic problem about sensitivity training is the 'so-what'
approach. 'All right, so the manager is more insightful, more aware,
more expressive, more open, more candid, listens better and so on, but
how does that really help get the work done?' The way to get the work
done, the argument runs, is to get the objectives set — management by
objectives. Unfortunately managing by objectives depends upon how
realistically the objectives are set which in turn depends upon the degree
of honesty and trust in the system. The method has been termed 'a do-it-
yourself hangman kit' and a number of firms have found it difficult to put
into practice.

A slightly condensed version of an article which appeared in Training and
Development Journal, January 1971.

The case study to be described in this chapter arose directly from such a failure; the client's concern with the results, or lack of results, produced by management by objectives. The training described is an attempt to build more effective interpersonal relationships among members of a working unit and to marry sensitivity training to objective-setting and role-clarification.

INITIAL CONSULTANT/CLIENT INTERACTION

The outside consultant was invited to a meeting between the client department and the Management Services Section. Those at the meeting consisted of senior managers from the department, experts in management by objectives from the Management Services Section, an adviser from the company headquarters and a divisional adviser on the implementation of organisational change.

The departmental manager outlined his organisation (see Figure 4:1) and gave some background to his present request for assistance. The department had recently been reorganised, not by managerial fiat but by an attempt at consultation and participation which had, in most instances, been favourably received by its members. The very success of the exercise together with the natural inclination of the departmental manager

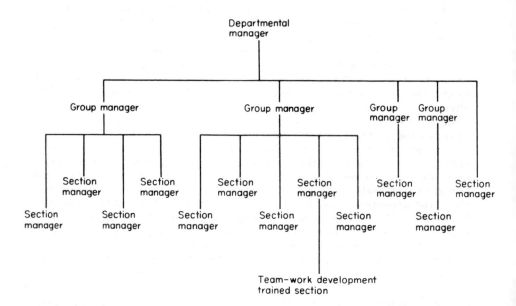

Figure 4:1   Department organisation chart

had led to pressure for further 'participative' management. How was this to be achieved? There were several alternatives; some members of the more senior management had been on a Managerial Grid phase 1 course (Blake and Mouton 1964) and the extension throughout the department to all levels was a clear possibility. Management by objectives had been implemented throughout one section within the department and although there were some reservations about its practice it was another possibility. Extensive and perhaps potentially risky delegation of authority had taken place in yet another section and this could serve as a model. The departmental manager was clearly strongly in favour of some sort of team building as a first step in extending his ideas on participative management, and he was in favour of training that emphasised the importance of inter-personal relations in task situations. The group manager whose sections were to be involved was much more hesitant about such an orientation and throughout the exercise stressed the need for training to be 'work-oriented'.

The group manager was strongly resistant to the open-ended nature of T-group type activities which he perceived to be the particular speciality of the consultant. One of the common problems of in-company T-groups is that the trainer may attempt to work at a level which the clients may find unacceptable : comments such as 'Let's keep personalities out of this' and 'Expressing our feelings about each other is going to get us nowhere fast' indicate commonly held resistances by managers. Although in some cases these may be little more than superficial initial reactions, it is considered important to avoid an inappropriate level of intervention (Harrison 1970) and little can be achieved by forcing people through a process to which there is resistance. Given this thinking and the initial resistance, the consultant explored the concern and was inclined to move towards a more structured approach.

On the other hand, the consultant was as resistant to a highly structured approach as the group manager was to a highly unstructured approach, and he particularly objected to the Blake & Mouton Managerial Grid which was being urged upon him, as he perceived it to lead to superficial responses. In his view a method like that of Reddin (1970) ran the risk of doing little more than establishing a new managerial jargon and effecting little real change in team relationships. He also argued that the precise and relatively rigid instrumentation involved in both the Blake and the Reddin approach could, in fact, reinforce the very conditions which the consultant was called in to change, since the instruments could be seen as controlling the areas of discussion and defining the problems for the participants. It could be argued that questionnaires and other devices are essentially mechanistic and ill-suited to the engendering of participative work groups and supportive task teams (Argyris 1968).

The interplay of the opposing forces of structure and non-structure resulted in an interesting compromise when the planning group eventually prepared and administered a questionnaire based on Blake. This questionnaire consisted of nine questions covering most aspects of how a team can work together : objectives, initiative, teamwork, conflict,

'HOW DOES YOUR TEAM WORK?'

QUESTIONNAIRE

Consider the way in which your team usually works : then tick the paragraph under (a), (b) or (c) under each main heading (for example, 'objectives') which most nearly describes how the team normally operates. Each main question has an explanatory introduction which we hope will make the question clear to you.

Objectives. When people have goals and objectives for which they are striving they have a clear sense of direction and their efforts are purposeful. They know in specific terms what they are trying to achieve. As a result they are likely to be more effective and get more satisfaction from their work than if they were just told what to do, or simply drifted along.
  Is your team one in which :

(a) Everyone has clearly understood goals and objectives which are used as standards to evaluate performance and which have a built-in time plan
(b) Specific goals and objectives are not established but most people have some idea of what they should achieve
(c) Goals and objectives do not exist or if they do they are ignored; individual or team performance is not thought of in terms of goals or objectives

Conflict. Whenever a group of people have to work together, conflict is inevitable because people are different, have different ideas, seek different things, have different views and so on. Sometimes there are straight disagreements on the interpretation of certain facts. Differences of opinion and differences of feeling are not in themselves bad or good — but unless these conflicts are opened up so that they can be worked through to a creative solution they can seriously disrupt team working.
  Is your team one in which :

(a) Real conflicts are faced up to in order to achieve solutions which meet with understanding and agreement
(b) Compromise solutions are sought because facing up to the problems causes too many bad feelings or might 'upset the applecart'
(c) Conflicts are 'swept under the carpet' in the hope that they will go away (instead of which they tend to pop up in unexpected places)

Figure 4:2   Extract from questionnaire given to course members creativity, communication, cost consciousness, planning and reviewing action.

Figure 4:2 gives a representative extract from the questionnaire.

It was a questionnaire with a difference : it was deliberately imprecise and non-elaborate. The aim was to build a flexible instrument which would grow as a result of the interaction between the section under development and the consulting staff.

The rationale behind the use of the participant-controlled questionnaire, apart from the pressure from the client, was derived from Harrison's (1965) work on support and confrontation. If an individual is to learn at all he must be provided with both 'a castle' into which he can retreat and 'a battlefield' where he can be faced with issues. In this instance, the questionnaire was the castle, the interpersonal, unstructured issues deriving from it, the battlefield. It was hoped that it would not become an end in itself, but simply a means to facilitate discussion. At the same time it could be used either by a group member to escape from the battle-field or by the consultant to refocus efforts on working towards objective setting. Throughout the exercise, therefore, and in subsequent writing-up of roles and objectives, the team members were encouraged to initiate new questions and new ideas, to alter drafts, to revise summaries and generally to make the instrumentation useful to themselves.

To further strengthen the participants' feeling of control and freedom from experimental manipulation, no evaluation instruments were included in the initial programme which is outlined in Figure 4:3.

TEAMWORK DEVELOPMENT IN ACTION

Naturally, in the course of the training much of the discussion centred on the personal needs of members of the section and on the nature of their working relationships with each other and must remain confidential. It is possible, however, to give some broad indications as to the development of the work.

The section consisted of eight people, ranging from a leader with a PhD and considerable experience, to a process trainee with no qualifications and only a few weeks' experience of the company to draw on. All meetings were held at the works.

Before the first meeting, each member had filled out the questionnaire and added his comments. It was intended that this data should be organised and fed back anonymously, but the members felt there was little to be gained by this and a great deal to be lost by people not owning their scores. A ground rule was agreed whereby people were not to be pressured to explain their scores if they didn't wish to and, with this proviso, answers were shared.

It came as a surprise to most members to discover that there was considerable difference in answers.

The next few hours were spent in working through the scores. Why had

Date	Activity	Rationale	Involved
25 November	1 Pre-work	1 Section manager and consultants discuss programme	Section manager and consultants
27 November 4 pm onwards	2 Pre-work	2 Individual section members work through the questionnaire, 'How does your team operate'. This gives raw data for the subsequent activities	Section members
28 November 8.45 am - 4.45 pm	3 Assessment of actual section culture	3 Use questionnaire to facilitate discussion which will lead to freeing up of interpersonal relationships, work-based problems, emotions, questions of status, etc. It is important that all team problems raised are explored and nothing is regarded as being out of court. 'Exercise Co-operation' (described on page 77) was used to assist discussion of section operation in terms of trust, openness, cooperation or conflict, etc.	Consultants, section manager and section members
29 November 8.45 am - 7 pm	4 Assessment of an ideal section culture	4 This uses the same multiple-choice format as for culture assessment; individuals do it first then the section agrees. Main point is to create a standard of excellence on which to base next step(s), but as always the discussion is material for learning	Consultants, section manager and section members
	5 Identification of barriers to excellence	5 This is the diagnostic phase in which inter- and intra-section difficulties are identified and possible means of solution discussed	Consultants, section manager and section members
	6 Review of activities and progress	6 Review progress so far and discuss any actions/refinements to be built into later stages	Consultants, group manager and section manager
Break			

Date	Activity	Rationale	Involved
13 December 8.45 am - 4.45 pm	7 Means of overcoming barriers to excellence	7 Through discussion, a list of problems and possible means of solution is set up. It is hoped that this will lead to 'work team development'	Consultants, section manager and section members
	8 Review of progress	8 Resource people and group and section managers review progress and finalise details of last stages	Consultants, group manager, section manager
Break			
16 and 17 December 8.45 am - 4.45 pm each day	9 'Work Team'	9 Conventional group activity as already practised, but with some reference to difficulties of an interpersonal nature, etc. based on previous learning. It is hoped that these will lead to clear role concepts and objectives for the section and individuals with commitment to them, job enlargements and a basis for continual review/improvement in performance	Consultants, section manager and section members
17 December	10 Progress	10 Resource people and group/ section managers review total exercise so far	
14 January 1969	11 Team review	11 Group manager and section manager review progress towards solutions of intra- and inter-group difficulties revealed during exercise	Consultants, group manager, section manager and section members

Figure 4:3   Initial programme for team training

discrepancies arisen? What specific events had shaped the respective images of the team? There was an initial reluctance to focus on the section itself; frequently scores were justified by examples drawn from outside groups — experiences in other teams in the department, experiences with other leaders in other teams at other times, but gradually the members began to talk about their current feelings, their own team, their experiences in it and the problems they had in its effective operation.

At the outset there was a marked degree of scepticism about working as a section team at all.

'I do my job and he does his, but I'm damned if there's any reason why I should go out of my way to help him.'

'There's no reason for us to have contact, we don't need each other ...'

'There's not one team here, there's three or four — in some instances eight.'

Comments such as these led to considerable discussion about what benefits, if any, could accrue from operating together rather than in twos or threes. A consensus was reached which accepted that whilst it was impossible and, perhaps, undesirable to find out completely what others were engaged in, there was certain a great deal to be gained from sharing information more fully and from sharing responsibilities more widely through the section.

A great deal of time was spent on this issue because it was considered to be the most fundamental. If there were to be latent feelings that operating as a team was not meaningful then the rest of the training would be irrelevant. In inviting the members to discuss this issue the consultant was epitomising the approach to be stressed throughout the training, that the working-through of problems was essential to effective relationships.

The question of working-through rather than backing-off became very prominent when the members focused on the reactions to the question on conflict. The scores revealed that nearly all the members considered it useful to 'let sleeping dogs lie'. There appeared to be strong feelings that conflict must be avoided whatever the personal costs. The consultant invited the members to give free associations around the notion of conflict and a very impressive list of negative connotations was generated: 'violence', 'destruction', 'vicious', 'cruel', 'hurt', 'smash', 'batter', 'war', 'fight', 'bitter struggle', 'immature squabble', etc. The implications of this negativism were discussed and a handout on conflict was distributed to reinforce the points made by the consultants ; conflict could be positive, issues could be worked through and resolved.

After some general conversation around the need for people to face up to problems, the consultant intervened :

'What does this discussion mean for this section here and now? What conflicts do we envisage in talking about the problems we have in working together?'

This intervention prompted an almost immediate return to the questionn-aire. Gradually, however, an atmosphere of openness and trust was being established. The development of this was greatly facilitated by the attitude of the section manager who was willing, as he rather unfortunately put it, 'to stick my neck on the block'. At several points he intervened to suggest that his role be discussed.

'I'm willing to listen to any comments. '

Both he and the members realised how difficult it was to discuss roles and relationships even though the consultant gave them support and encouraged them to comment on each other's actions in an essentially non-evaluative fashion. They were encouraged to say, 'What you did made me feel such and such a feeling,' rather than bluntly saying, 'What you did was stupid, wrong, wicked, etc.' In the former manner it was stressed that the recipient was more likely to <u>hear</u> the comment, could test his intentions against the reality fed back to him by the respondent and could modify his future behaviour if he <u>chose to do so</u>.

Listening to what others said, of course, was bound up with how they presented what they had to say, but listening in itself was a central concern of the consultant's interventions. Members realised how little they listened when they were challenged by the consultant to repeat the other man's argument before they attempted to counter it. Such interventions led to a marked improvement in mutual attention, to an improvement in <u>really</u> hearing what the other had to say rather than seizing upon points on which he could be attacked.

At the beginning of the second day, a non-verbal exercise was introduced to stress the value of working together. Building upon the previous sessions the consultants encouraged the group to discuss cooperation and then to conduct an experiment in it. The exercise involved five envelopes in each of which there were a number of pieces of cardboard for forming squares. The group's task was to form five squares of equal size, but there were some specific limitations imposed upon the group (Nylen 1967).

1   No member may speak
2   No member may ask another member for a cardboard piece or in any way signal that another person is to give him a piece
3   Members may, however, give cards to other members

The team worked well on the problem and had it completed within ten minutes and then focused upon their feelings during the exercise. One member spoke of how he felt the urge to grab pieces and arrange them for another; another spoke of his insecurity at being under scrutiny by his colleagues and the consultants; another spoke of his frustration at not being able to point out 'the obvious' to the person he was sitting next to. The section manager observed that he had completed his square very early on and had sat back satisfied. 'It's only now', he continued, 'that I realise I never thought of giving any or all of it away'.

The consultant asked if the game had any relevance to his work situation. 'Are you referring to delegation?' asked the manager. 'Do I give any of my power and responsibility to anyone else? Well, I think I go further than most, but what do the others think?' This opened up the whole area of job enlargement and job enrichment and led to a discussion of personal career needs and organisation obstacles to their fulfilment.

This was really the take-off point for an extensive discussion of roles and objectives and it was on this base that the management by objectives specialist was able to build subsequently. Sufficient trust had developed within the section for members to begin to share their views about the jobs, their relationships and the company. This opening up was further facilitated by the use of another simple exercise where members were invited to speak about work-related satisfactions and dissatisfactions. 'What gives you happiness and sense of achievement?' 'What causes you anxiety, irritation and frustrations?' Each took his turn with an egg-timer which symbolised the right to speak uninterrupted for six minutes, and there were some very frank and non-superficial comments. One theme ran through many of the contributions — the need to be considered:

'I know I'm pretty unimportant to this organisation, but I would just like sweetening up a little at times. Just like to feel that what I am doing is appreciated.'

'I like to feel that I am being trusted. It's more important to be given that impression than to get on, for me anyway ...'

'In the selling job I did, I was given complete freedom, I was trusted by the company and accepted by the customer ...'

'I like to think somebody cares about what I'm doing ...'

Over the next few hours a number of problems were explored and feelings discussed; the inter-unit problems of laboratory-based and office-based staff were discussed and suggestions made for resolution; the attitudes to transfers and career development were analysed; the desire for full monthly technical discussions rather than daily 'courtesy' visits was put forward; the assessment scheme was reviewed and suggestions made for its revision; communications within and outside the section were examined and found wanting; suggestions were made for improvement.

A summary of the major actions agreed upon was made by the section manager and the internal consultant and circulated to the members with a letter: 'Attached is a summary of the actions agreed at the team development session held recently ... It has been prepared by myself from the notes we made at the last meeting, but there may well be parts with which you disagree or items that you feel should be added. Please consider this document as a DRAFT; scribble on it, rewrite it, do anything you like with it, but don't regard it as sacred.'

Taking this revised summary as a guide the section manager and the individual members completed their individual roles and objectives using 'modified' management by objectives techniques.

The modified form of management by objectives work differed significantly from the traditional form in that team relationships rather than the pure boss-subordinate relationship were concentrated on. Also the actual technique was very much simplified, dealing only with statements of role and objectives rather than the elaborate system of key areas, key tasks, performance standards, means of monitoring performances, etc. used in a traditional approach.

The management by objectives part of the exercise basically fell into two parts. First the whole section, following on their previous discussions, established their overall section role with particular reference to the technical areas of their work and then discussed and allocated amongst themselves the technical areas of work. During this stage, ideas on job enlargement and enrichment, arising from the earlier discussions, were firmed up and built into the work allocation.

The second part involved the members individually : each in turn, with the assistance of the internal consultant, drafted his personal roles and objectives based on all the previous discussions. Deliberately the drafting of roles and objectives commenced with the most junior people and then on up through the team. This was to ensure that individuals had maximum opportunity for seeking job enlargement.

Finally when all members had their roles and objectives, a section meeting was held to establish that there were no conflicting roles or objectives, duplication, etc. This resulted in a few minor amendments, mainly in the area of objectives rather than roles, so that objectives meshed better.

EVALUATION

As mentioned earlier, no formal evaluation instruments were built into the programme. Nonetheless, at the outset some general objectives were given to the consultant :

1   To have raised the effectiveness of the section through the greater personal involvement of the staff in the managerial process.
2   To have fostered frank and open team working and a full commitment to the continual review/improvement of the section performance.

At the same time as these general objectives were given, some evaluation criteria were suggested :

1   The ability of the team to create, select and progress projects.
2   Improved morale and team working of section members.
3   The ability of the section to relate its manning requirements to its work loading.
4   The effectiveness of work planning to cover the absence of senior staff.
5   The amount of delegation/job enlargement which had taken place.

How far was the exercise successful in meeting the objectives and how does it measure up against the criteria? These are difficult questions to answer but the subjective opinions of both the group manager and the departmental manager are that both the objectives were met. They also noted a marked increase in morale and a much greater willingness of the members to work together.

A good example of the process in action, and in itself a measure of the team's progress, occurred at a late stage of the training. During January 1969 an 'instruction' had been circulated to all containing words and phrases which the team as a whole thought ran contrary to their newly acquired participative style. In a special meeting they discussed the document with the group manager and fed back their reactions. Though he had not taken part in the training exercise, they were able to give him very direct comments on how the document had been received throughout the department. It was notable that they managed to avoid attack and anger. Though the group manager had not anticipated difficulty with this particular document, he was able to appreciate the feelings it had provoked, and the team was able to accept that it had not been his intention to be seen as laying down the law unilaterally. All eventually agreed that the ideas in the 'instruction' were sound.

The section itself built in work planning in its objective setting to cover the absence of more senior staff and, as indicated above, since the drafting of roles and objectives began with the most junior people and worked up, job enlargement had taken place. At the time of writing, no formal review of progress had taken place, so there is no information available on the ability of the section to create, select and progress projects, nor is there any information on the ability of the section to relate its manning requirements to its work load.

Therefore, on three of the five criteria the exercise would seem to have been a success, so much so that the department has now made plans to follow up the initial pilot study with further exercises throughout the other sections. It would appear that, at least in this circumstance, there is no reason why both management by objectives and sensitivity training cannot work.

It has to be borne in mind that, for the leader, it is relatively unthreatening to manage a submissive team, but it can cause him a great deal of anxiety to be faced with a more 'participative' group. It would appear essential that the degree of participation be spelled out before the development of teams is undertaken. People who are encouraged to become more involved and more committed will ask demanding questions and will expect answers. If the top management is not clear about why it wants teams developed — to what end and within what limits — then it could conceivably arrive at a situation where the organisation suffers an overall lowering of satisfaction, morale and effectiveness.

A further related point needs to be made. It would be quite unreasonable to expect a five-day intervention to affect the habits of interaction built up over the years. It would also be unrealistic to expect trained teams to present no problems. Groups unused to freedom of discussion are not going to open up (Likert 1961). Short-term gain, therefore, is out of the question and long-term benefit is only possible if the training is consistent with some overall plan of organisation development.

So, much training needs to be undertaken on faith and perhaps much of it is merely fashionable. Nonetheless, it was not a theoretician nor a contemporary who wrote :

'Since the general introduction of inanimate mechanism into British manufactures, man, with few exceptions, had been treated as a secondary and inferior machine; and far more attention has been given to perfect the raw materials of wood and metals than those of the body and mind. Give but due reflection to this subject, and you will find that man, even as an instrument for the creation of wealth, may still be greatly improved.

'But, my friends, a far more interesting and gratifying consideration remains. Adopt the means which erelong shall be rendered obvious to every understanding, and you may not only partially improve those living instruments, but learn how to impart to them such excellence as shall make them infinitely surpass those of the present and all former times.'

It was Robert Owen in the early nineteenth century.

REFERENCES

Argyris, C (1968) 'Some unintended consequences of rigorous research', Psychological Bulletin, 70, 185-97.

Blake, R R & Mouton, J S (1964) The Managerial Grid (Houston Texas, Gulf Publishing)

Campbell, J P and Dunnette, M D (1968) 'Effectiveness of T-group experiences in managerial training and development', Psychological Bulletin, 70, 73-104.

Friedlander, F (1966) 'Performance and interactional dimensions of organisational work groups', Journal of Applied Psychology, 50, 257-65.

Friedlander, F (1968) 'A comparative study of consulting processes and group development', Journal of Applied Behavioural Science, 4, 377-99.

Harrison, R (1965) Cognitive Models for Interpersonal and Group Behaviour (Explorations in Human Relations Training and Research, number 2) (Washington DC, National Training Laboratories).

Harrison, R (1970) 'Choosing the depth of organisation intervention', Journal of Applied Behavioural Science, 6, 181-202.

Likert, R (1961) New Patterns of Management (New York, McGraw-Hill)

Mangham, I L and Cooper, C (1969) 'The impact of T-groups on managerial behaviour', Journal of Management Studies, 6, 53-72.

Nylen, D (1967) Handbook of Training (NTL/EIT)

Pugh, D (1965) 'T-group training from the point of view of organization theory', in T-group Training : Group Dynamics in Management Education (Oxford, Basil Blackwell).

Reddin, W J (1970) Managerial Effectiveness (London, McGraw-Hill).

5

Role negotiation: a tough-minded approach to team development

by Roger Harrison

Behavioural-science approaches to business have tended to focus on
alternatives to power and politics in management and decision-making,
rather than directly upon the influence process. In the United States, for
example, the sensitivity-training approach has had quite a vogue. Managers
are encouraged to abandon competitiveness and manipulation of one another
in favour of open discussion of feelings, collaboration based on mutual
trust, and egalitarian approaches to decision-making. Various techniques
(the T-group, the Managerial Grid) have been developed to bring about
these changes.

In other approaches managers have been urged to change the motivational
system, moving from reliance upon monetary rewards and punishments
towards the development of more internal motivation based upon intrinsic
interest in the job, and personal commitment to meeting work objectives.
Examples are programmes of job enrichment and management by
objectives. Still other practitioners have developed purely rational approaches
to group problem-solving (for example, Kepner Tregoe in the United States
and Coverdale in Britain).

In these approaches, competition, conflict and the struggle for power and
influence tend to be explained away or ignored. They assume people will be
collaborative and productive if they are taught how or if the barriers to
their doing so are removed. These approaches may be called tender minded
in that they see power struggle as a symptom or a managerial mistake

rather than as a basic and ubiquitous process in organisations. The problem of organisational change is seen as one of releasing human potential for collaboration and productivity, rather than as one of controlling or checking competition for advantage and position. Of course this is not true of all behavioural approaches without exception. One in particular which has influenced my own thinking in the development of role negotiation is the 'confrontation meeting' developed by Richard Beckhard some years ago.

Consider some examples of problems from the author's personal experience in a consulting practice.

A product-centred system has been installed by a company which is organised along traditional functional lines. The product group includes representatives from the relevant functional divisions (sales, marketing, production, engineering, research, etc). One group meets under the chairmanship of a product manager to review the commercial performance of the product and to plan capital expenditure, cost and production targets, pricing and marketing strategy. In practice, however, some of the product managers call very few meetings and prepare the product plans without much input or consultation from the functional members of the group. The latter feel they have insufficient influence over the final target figures which they are called upon to meet and that the figures are frequently 'unrealistic'. Their performance frequently falls short of the target.

The production and engineering managers of a works have frequent disagreements over the work that is done by the latter for the former. The production manager complains that the engineering manager sets maintenance priorities to meet his own convenience and reduce his own costs, rather than to make sure production targets are met. The engineering manager maintains that the production manager gives insufficient notice of jobs which can be foreseen, and that the production operators cause unnecessary breakdowns by failure to carry out preventive maintenance procedures faithfully. The two men have aired their dissatisfactions with one another's performance from time to time, but both agree that no significant change has occurred.

A scientist in a development department complains of overly close supervision by his section manager. The scientist says that the manager intervenes to change the priorities that he assigns to work, to interfere with his development of promising lines of inquiry, and that the manager checks up with insulting frequency to see that his instructions are being carried out. The scientist is actively trying to get a transfer to another section, because he feels he cannot do a proper job with so much hampering interference from above. When interviewed, the section manager says the scientist does competent work but is secretive and unwilling to listen to advice. He fails to let the manager know what he is doing and deviates without discussion from agreements the manager thought they had about how the work would be carried out. The manager feels he has to spend far too much time checking up on the scientist and is beginning to wonder whether his otherwise good work is worth the trouble which is required to manage him.

Each of these examples describes a problem involving the power and influence of one person or group over the activities of another. In each one, the objective of one or both parties is to gain increased control over the actions of the other, reduce control by the other over his own activities, or both at once. What is more, the participants themselves see the problem as one of influence and power. A consultant might tell them that their trouble was one of communication, or objective setting, or rational problem solving, and they would listen politely and perhaps try the approach suggested by the expert. But in their hearts they would still feel it was a question of who was going to have the final say, who was going to be boss.

Although my development as a consultant was very much in the tender-minded tradition, I have increasingly come to feel that these managers are right. My growing conviction is that my clients have a more accurate mental map of the forces affecting them in their organisational lives than my academic colleagues have. This map usually charts power and influence, and whether people are on their side or against them. On the map are indications as to whom one can be open and honest with, and who will use the information against one. My clients do not chart an organisational world which is safe for openness, collaboration, creativity and personal growth.

I do not mean to imply that the more optimistic behavioural-science approaches to business are so naive as to claim the world is quite safe for the processes they try to promote. What is of concern is the failure to work with the forces which _are_ in ascendance. This chapter presents a modest programme for working with human problems in organisations which does work directly with issues of power, competitiveness and coercion. The use of this method also involves an attempt to work from the clients' views of their problems and situations without making assumptions in advance about what their 'real' needs are. This programme is based on 'role negotiation', a technique which has been found useful in resolving differences and conflicts between managers and subordinates, between co-workers, and between different groups in an organisation.

The name of the technique describes the process, which involves changing by means of negotiation with other interested parties the _role_ which an individual or group performs in the organisation. By an individual's or group's 'role' is meant the work arrangements he has with the others : what activities he is supposed to perform, what decisions he can make, to whom he reports and about what and how often, who can legitimately tell him what to do and under what circumstances, and so on. Some people would say that a man's job is the same as what is called here his role, and this is partially true. But what is meant by role includes not only the formal job description, but also all the informal understandings, agreements, expectations and arrangements with others which determine the way one person's or group's work affects or fits in with another's.

The basic approach of role negotiation has been successfully used with a wide variety of situations and clients : for example, a top-management work team, a small teaching faculty, a large group of school administrators, superior/subordinate pairs, a special project team. It has even proved useful in working with marital disagreements between husbands and wives, and can be regarded as a more or less universal tool for conflict resolution. The technique can be used with very small or quite large groups, although it is well to break down into subgroups if the size is over eight to ten. The technique has been administered with fifty or sixty people at one time, where they worked in smaller units which brought together those people who had the most to do with each other on the job.

The technique makes one basic assumption: that most people prefer a fair negotiated settlement to a state of unresolved conflict, and that they are willing to invest some time and make some concessions in order to achieve a solution. To operate the programme, a modest but significant risk is called for from the participants: they must be open about what changes in behaviour, authority, responsibility, etc. they wish to obtain from others in the situation. If the participants take the risk asked of them and specify concretely the changes desired on the part of others, then significant changes in work effectiveness can usually be obtained.

STAGES OF A ROLE-NEGOTIATION PROGRAMME

For the sake of illustration, it will be assumed that a consultant is working with a group of five to seven people which includes a manager and his subordinates, two levels in the formal organisation.

Preparation

It goes almost without saying that no interference into the work relationships of a group or organisation will be very successful unless the participants have confidence in the motives and competence of the consultant and are therefore willing at his behest to try something new and a bit strange. It also stands to reason that the consultant should know enough about the people, their work system and their relationship problems to satisfy himself that the members of the group are ready to make a real effort towards improvement. No technique will work if the clients do not trust the consultant enough to give it a fair try or if the members of the group (particularly the highly influential members) devote most of their effort to maintaining the status quo. In what follows it will be assumed that this confidence and readiness to work have been established. It is realised that this is a rather large assumption, but these problems are universal in consulting and not peculiar to role negotiation. If anything, I have found that role negotiation requires somewhat less preparation than other team-development techniques used in the past.

Time and place

If these basics are out of the way, an effort is made to have at least a day with the group away from the job location to get the role-negotiation process under way. Half-day exercises have been conducted but they were more in the nature of demonstrations than actual working sessions. A two-day session with a commitment to follow up in three to four weeks is about optimum. If the group is not felt to be quite prepared to undertake serious work, the session may be made longer with some trust-building and diagnostic activities in the beginning, working into the role negotiation when and if the group is ready for it.

The consulting contract

The first step in the actual role negotiation is <u>contract setting</u>. Its purpose is to get clear between the group and the consultant what each may expect from the other. This is a critical step in the change process. It controls and channels everything which happens afterwards. A contract should be worked towards with the following provisions which are best written down as a first practice step in the rather formal way of working which is established.

1   It is not legitimate for the consultant to press or probe anyone's <u>feelings</u>. The group is concerned about work : who does what, how and with whom. How people <u>feel</u> about their work or about others in the group is their own business, to be introduced or not according to their own judgement and desire. The expression of feelings is not part of the contract.

2   Openness and honesty about behaviour is expected and is essential for the achievement of results. This means that the consultant will probe people to be specific and concrete in expressing their expectations and demands for the behaviour of others. Each team member is expected to be open and specific about what he wants others to <u>do more</u> or <u>do better</u> or <u>do less</u> or <u>maintain unchanged</u>.

3   No expectation or demand is adequately communicated until it has been <u>written down</u> and is clearly understood by both sender and receiver, nor will any change process be engaged in until this has been done.

4   The full sharing of expectations and demands does not constitute a completed change process. It is only the precondition for change to be agreed through negotiation. It is unreasonable for anyone in the group, manager or subordinate, to expect that any change will take place merely as a result of communicating a demand or expectation. Unless a team member is willing to change his own behaviour in order to get what he wants from the other(s), he is likely to waste his and the group's time talking about the issue. When a member makes a request or demand for changed behaviour on the part of another, the consultant will always ask what <u>quid pro quo</u> (something for something) he is willing to give in order

to get what he wants. This goes for the manager as well as for the sub-ordinates. If the former can get what he wants simply by issuing orders or clarifying expectations from his position of authority, he probably does not need a consultant or a change process.

5   The change process is essentially one of bargaining and negotiation in which two or more members each agree to change behaviour in exchange for some desired change on the part of the other. This process is not complete until the agreement can be written down in terms which include the agreed changes in behaviour and make clear what each party is expected to give in return.

6   Threats and pressures are neither illegitimate nor excluded from the negotiation process. However, group members should realise that over-reliance on threats and punishment usually results in defensiveness, concealment, decreased communication and retaliation, and may lead to breakdown of the negotiation. The consultant will do his best to help members to accomplish their aims with positive incentives wherever possible.

During the discussion of the contract, the consultant helps participants see that each member has power and influence in the group, both positively to reward and collaborate with others, and negatively to resist, block or punish. Each uses his power and influence to create a desirable and satisfying work situation for himself. When this process takes place covertly, people often use a lot of time and energy on it unproductively. It is unproductive because people are unsure about others' desires and intentions. This makes it difficult to judge how a particular action will be responded to. We often judge others' wants and needs as though they were like our own. We 'do unto others as we would have them do unto us' and, because they are not in all respects like us, our ignorance results in ineffectiveness. We make guesses about how others will respond to our attempts to influence their behaviour and when the guesses are wrong, we have no option other than to continue the laborious process of trial and error, slowly building up our knowledge of what is and is not effective with each other person through a clumsy and not very systematic experimentation.

    In stable, slowly changing organisational situations, this trial and error process may be satisfactory, because people do learn how to influence one another effectively. The effort is made to help clients to see that if information about desires and intentions is equally shared, then they will all increase the effectiveness of their influence attempts. Then, when others try to influence them the proffered quid pro quo will be more likely to be one which they really want and need. The role negotiation is not only intended to have the effect of resolving current problems but also of increasing knowledge within the group of how effectively to influence one another. The intended effect is that the total amount of influence of group members on one another should increase. The consultant will so conduct himself that opportunities to increase one's influence within the system are as nearly equal as possible.

Diagnosis

The next stage is _issue diagnosis_. Each member is asked to spend some time thinking about the way business is conducted between himself and the others in the group. What things would he change if he could? What things would he like to keep as they are? Who and what would have to change in order to improve things? In thinking about these things, the members are asked to focus especially on the things which might be changed to improve their _own effectiveness_, as these are the things they will be asked to discuss and negotiate.

After they have spent twenty minutes or so thinking about these matters and perhaps making a few notes, each member is asked to take a set of issue diagnosis forms like the one in Figure 5:1. He is asked to fill out one issue diagnosis form for each other member, listing those things he would like to see the other person:

1   Do more or do better
2   Do less or stop doing
3   Keep on doing, maintain unchanged

All of these messages are to be directed towards increasing the sender's own effectiveness in doing his own job.

These lists are exchanged so that each person has all the lists which pertain to his work behaviour. Each member makes a master list for himself on a large piece of (flip chart) paper on which he shows the behaviour which each other person desires him to do _more_ or _better_, _less_ or _continue unchanged_ (see Figure 5:2). These are posted so that the entire group can peruse and refer to each list. Each member is allowed to question the others who have sent messages about his behaviour, querying the what? why? and how? of their requests, but no one is allowed a rebuttal, defence or even a yes-or-no reply to the messages he has received. The consultant intervenes in the discussion to make sure that only clarification is taking place and that argument, discussion and decision-making about issues is not engaged in at this stage.

The purpose of this rather rigid and formal control on communication by the consultant is to make sure that the group does not have a negative problem-solving experience and that members do not get polarised on issues or take up extreme positions which they will feel impelled to defend in order to save face. Communication is controlled in order to prevent escalation of actual or potential conflicts. The strategy is to channel the energy which has been generated or released by the sharing of demands and expectations into successful problem solving and mutual influence. The consultant intervenes to inhibit hostile and destructive expression at this point and later to facilitate constructive bargaining and negotiation of

1   IF YOU WERE TO DO THE FOLLOWING THINGS <u>MORE</u> or <u>BETTER</u>,
    IT WOULD HELP ME TO INCREASE MY OWN EFFECTIVENESS

    'Be more receptive to improvement suggestions from the process
    engineers.

    Give <u>help</u> on cost control (see 2).

    Fight harder with the G M to get our plans improved.'

2   IF YOU WERE TO DO THE FOLLOWING THINGS <u>LESS,</u> OR WERE
    TO <u>STOP</u> DOING THEM, IT WOULD HELP ME TO INCREASE MY
    OWN EFFECTIVENESS

    'Acting as judge and jury on cost control.

    Checking up frequently on small details of the work -
    asking for so many detailed progress reports.'

3   THE FOLLOWING THINGS WHICH YOU HAVE BEEN DOING HELP
    TO INCREASE MY EFFECTIVENESS, AND I HOPE YOU WILL
    CONTINUE TO DO THEM

    'Passing on full information in our weekly meetings.

    Being available when I need to talk to you. '

Figure 5:1   Issue diagnosis form

MORE OR BETTER	LESS OR STOP	CONTINUE AS NOW
Give information on project progress completion date slippage — Bill, Tony, David.	Let people go to other good job opportunities — stop hanging on to your good engineers — Tony, Bill.	Training operators on preventive maintenance — Henry.
Send progress reports on Sortair project — Bill.	Missing weekly planning meetings frequently — Jack, Henry, David.	Good suggestions in meetings — Tony, Henry.
Make engineers more readily available when help needed — Jack, Henry.	Ignoring memos and reports re cost control — David.	Asking the difficult and awkward questions — Tony, Jack.
Keep better informed re plans and activities — David.	Setting aside my priorities on engineering work — Henry, Jack.	Willingness to help on design problems — Bill, Jack.
Enforce safety rules on engineers when in Production area — Henry.	Charging time on Sortair to other accounts — David.	Good-quality project work — Bill, Henry, David, Jack.
Push harder on the Sensitex project — David, Henry, Tony, Jack.	Over-running agreed project budget without discussing beforehand — David.	

Figure 5:2   Summary of messages
to James Farrell from other group members

mutually beneficial agreements. This initial sharing of desires and change
goals leads to a point at which the team development process is most
vulnerable, because if sufficient anger and defensiveness are generated by
the problem sharing, the consultant will not be able to hold the negative
processes in check long enough for the development of the positive problem-
solving spiral on which the process depends for its effectiveness. It is
true that such an uncontrollable breakthrough of hostility has not yet
occurred in experience with the method. Nevertheless, concern over the
negative possibilities is in part responsible for the slow, deliberate and
rather formal development of the confrontation of issues within the group.

Negotiation

After each member has had an opportunity to clarify the messages he has received, the group proceeds to the selection of issues for negotiation. The consultant begins this phase by re-emphasising that unless a <u>quid pro quo</u> can be offered in return for a desired behaviour change, there is little point in having a discussion about it : <u>unless behaviour changes on both sides, the most likely prediction is that the status quo will continue.</u> (It can be argued that this is an extremely conservative point of view and that behaviour does in fact change between men of good will simply as a result of an exchange of views. While it is not denied that this occurs, it is not assumed in practice and is a pleasant surprise when it happens!)

Each participant is asked to indicate one or more issues on which he particularly wants to get some change on the part of another. He is also asked to select one or more issues on which he feels it may be possible for him to move in the direction desired by others. He does this by marking his own flip chart and those of the other members. In effect, each person is indicating the issues upon which he most wants to exert influence and those on which he is most willing to accept influence. With the help of the consultant the group then goes through the lists to select the 'most negotiable issues': those where there is a combination of a high desire for change on the part of an initiator and a willingness to negotiate on the part of the person whose behaviour is the target of the change attempt. The consultant asks for a group of two or more persons who are involved in one such issue to volunteer for a negotiation demonstration before the rest of the group.

The negotiation process consists of the parties making contingent offers to one another of the form, 'If you do X, I will do Y.' The negotiation ends when all parties are satisfied that they will receive a reasonable return for whatever they are agreeing to give. The consultant asks that the agreement be formalised by writing down specifically and concretely what each party is going to give and receive in the bargain (Figure 5:3). He also asks the participants to discuss openly what sanctions can be applied in the case of nonfulfilment of the bargain by one or another party. Often this involves no more than reversion to the status quo, but it may involve the application of pressures and penalties as well.

After the negotiation demonstration the members are asked to select other issues they wish to work on. A number of negotiations may go on simultaneously, the consultant being involved at the request of any party to any negotiation. All agreements are published to the entire group, however, and questioned by the consultant and the other members to test the good faith and reality orientation of the parties in making them. Where agreement proves impossible, the consultant and other group members try to help the parties find further incentives (positive or, less desirably, coercive) which they may bring to bear to encourage agreement.

This process is, of course, not so simple as the bare bones outlined here. All kinds of difficulties can occur, from bargaining in bad faith, to

Jim agrees to let David know as soon as agreed completion dates and cost projections look as though they won't be met, and also to discuss each project's progress fully with David on a bi-weekly basis.

In return David agrees not to raise questions about details and completion dates, pending a trial of this agreement to see if it provides sufficient information soon enough to deal with questions from above.

Figure 5:3   Final written agreement
between James Farrell and David Sills

refusal to bargain at all, to escalation of conflict. Through personal experience, however, group members tend to be rather wise about the issues they can and cannot deal with, and the consultant should refrain from pushing them to negotiate issues they feel are unresolvable. The aim is to create a beginning to team development with a successful experience which group members will see as a fruitful way of improving their effectiveness and satisfaction. No attempt is made to go further than the members feel is reasonable.

Follow-up

At the conclusion of a team development cycle as outlined above, it is suggested that the group test the firmness of the agreements they have negotiated by living with them a while before trying to go further. They can then get together later to review the agreements, renegotiate ones which have not held or which are no longer viable, and continue the team development process by dealing with new issues. Hopefully, the group will eventually take over the conduct of the role-negotiation activity and the consultant's role will wither away. This can occur when the group has developed sufficient control over the dangers, avoidances and threats involved in the negotiation process that they no longer need third-party protection or encouragement. However, unusual success in freeing clients from dependence on the consultant's services is not claimed. What is found is that there is less backsliding between visits in teams using this method than when more interpersonally oriented change interventions are applied. The agreements obtained through role negotiation seem to have more 'teeth' in them than those which rely on the softer processes of interpersonal trust and openness.

THE DYNAMICS OF ROLE NEGOTIATION

Role negotiation intervenes directly into the relationships of power, authority and influence within the group. The change effort is directed at the work relationships among members. It avoids probing into the likes and dislikes of members for one another and their personal feelings about one another. In this it is more consonant with the task-oriented norms of business than are most other behavioural approaches. I have found that groups with whom there was difficulty working when the focus was on interpersonal issues dropped their resistance and turned willingly to problem solving when the approach was shifted to role negotiation.

When the technique was first developed, it was tried out on a client group which was proving particularly hard to work with. They were suspicious of each other and said quite openly that talking about their relationships was both 'irrelevant to our work problems' and 'dangerous — it could split the group apart.' When role negotiation was introduced to them they saw ways they could deal with things which were bothering them without getting into touchy emotional confrontations they could not handle. They dropped their resistance dramatically and turned to work with a will that was a surprise and delight.

This experience has been repeated more than once. Clients seem more at home with problems of power and influence than they do with interpersonal issues. They feel more competent and less dependent upon the skill and trustworthiness of the consultant in dealing with these issues and so they are ready to work sooner and harder. It was found that the consultant's skill was not so central to the change process as it is when dealing with interpersonal issues. The amount of skill and professional training which is required to conduct role negotiation is less than for more sensitive approaches.

That is not to say that role negotiation poses no threat to organisation members. The consultant asks participants to be open about matters which are often covert in normal life. This requires more than the normal amount of trust and confidence. If it did not, these matters would have been talked about before the group ever got to the role negotiation.

There seems also to be some additional discomfort involved in <u>writing down</u> the changes one would like to see another make in his work behaviour. Several times clients have questioned the necessity of doing this, and one suspects that some have avoided role negotiation altogether because this aspect made them uneasy. It is perhaps that one feels so <u>exposed</u> when one's concerns are written out for all to see, and there is the fear that others will think them silly, childish or odd (though this never seems to happen). If the matter comes up, it is pointed out that one need not write down <u>all</u> the concerns one has, but only those one would like to work on with others at this time.

Role negotiation, like any other process which really changes relationships, threatens people in one basic way: they are never quite sure they will personally be better off after the change than before. In the case of role negotiation, most of these fears revolve around losing power and influence, or losing freedom and becoming more controlled by others. There is particular resistance to talking openly about issues where one is trying for his own advantage to manipulate another, or when he feels that he might want to do this in the future. This could be the main reason clients in role negotiation so often try to avoid the step of writing down their agreements. They feel if things are not down in black and white it will be easier later on to ignore the agreement if it becomes inconvenient. Also, writing down agreements is contrary to the aura of trust and good fellowship which some groups like to create on the surface and under cover of which they engage in quite a lot of cut-throat competition.

Role negotiation is no panacea for power problems in groups and between people. People may bargain in bad faith; agreements once reached may be broken; circumstances and personnel may change so that the work done becomes irrelevant. However, these problems can exist in any group or organisation. What role negotiation does is to try to deal with the problems directly and to identify and use constructively those areas of mutual advantage where both sides can benefit from discussion and agreement. These areas are almost always larger than people think they are, and when they find that they can achieve something for themselves by open negotiation which they could not achieve by covert competition, then the more constructive process can begin to grow.

THE ECONOMICS OF ROLE NEGOTIATION

One disadvantage of most behavioural approaches to team development is that the level of skill and experience demanded of the consultant is very high indeed. Managers are not confident in dealing with these issues. Because they feel at risk they reasonably want to have as much safety and skill as money can buy. The demand for skilled consultants on interpersonal and group processes has created a shortage and a meteoric rise in consulting fees. It seems unlikely that the supply will soon catch up with the demand.

The shortage of highly skilled workers in team development suggests that ways should be found of lowering the amount of skill required for effective consultant performance. Role negotiation is seen as a way of reducing the skill requirements for team development consultation. Preliminary results by internal consultants using the approach have been promising. For example, one management development manager teamed up with a colleague to conduct a successful role negotiation with his own top management. He reported that the main problem was getting up the confidence to take on the job. The team development session itself went smoothly. It cannot be said whether this experience was typical; one suspects it was not. It does lead one to hope that role negotiation will prove to be practical for use by internal consultants without professional training in the behavioural sciences.

SUMMARY

The following comments highlight the aspects of role negotiation which
commend it for use in team development and other face-to-face consulting
situations in business.

Role negotiation focuses on work relationships : what people do, and
how they facilitate and inhibit one another in the performance of their jobs.
It encourages participants to work with problems using words and concepts
they are using in business. It avoids probing to the deeper levels of their
feelings about one another unless this comes out naturally in the process.

Role negotiation deals directly with problems of power and influence
which may be neglected by other behavioural approaches. It does not
attempt to dethrone the authority in the group, but other members are
helped to explore realistically the sources of power and influence available
to them.

Role negotiation is highly action oriented in contrast to some other
behavioural approaches to team development. Its aim is not just the
exposing and understanding of issues as such, but the achievement of
commitment to changed ways of working through mutually negotiated
agreements. Changes achieved through role negotiation thus tend to be
more stable and lasting than where such a commitment procedure is lacking.

All the procedures of role negotiation are clear and simple, if a bit
mechanical, and can be described to clients in advance so they know what
they are getting into. There is nothing mysterious about the technique, and
this reduces clients' feelings of dependency upon the special skill of the
consultant.

Role negotiation actually requires less skill from the consultant than
some other behavioural approaches. It is suitable for use without lengthy
special training by internal consultants who are not themselves behavioural
scientists. It can therefore be a moderate-cost approach to organisational
change.

One final comment on the relationship between role negotiation and other
behavioural approaches is in order. As mentioned above, my own
development as a consultant was in the tradition of sensitivity training and
other 'soft' approaches to organisational change. I believed then and still
do that work groups can be effective and achievement oriented and at the
same time can support open and deeply satisfying interpersonal relationships among the members. What I do not now believe is that approaches
at the interpersonal level can work well unless the ever-present issues of
power and influence are first resolved to a reasonable level of satisfaction
for the members. Role negotiation was not designed as a substitute for
interpersonal approaches, but rather to fill this gap and provide a sound
and effective base upon which to build more satisfying relationships. As a
first or 'basic' approach to team development, I think it is more appropriate
than the more interpersonally focused methods. But I would hope that client
groups would develop that commitment to their own growth and development
which will eventually move them beyond role negotiation into deeper

exploration of their own creative potential for integrating work and
relationship.

6

Group training and consultancy approaches in IBM UK Ltd

by Alan Drinkwater

This chapter is a record of the progress made in the central management development department at IBM in developing approaches for improving social skills both of individual managers and of groups within the Company. It traces some of the learning steps we have undergone to arrive at our current stage of development and describes the people responsible.

The introduction is intended as a stage setter to the three succeeding sections, the first of which describes a training approach for developing individual skills and skills for working in groups, called 'action training'. The next section describes a training approach for developing an understanding of inter-group relationships within an organisation, an 'organisation laboratory'. The training designs of these two sections are based upon courses for non-reporting managers. The third section describes a 'team-building' approach aimed at improving effectiveness of groups of managers in reporting relationships at their normal meetings.

During the 1950s and 1960s IBM UK Limited, a subsidiary of an American company of similar name, grew from a company with a few hundred employees to one with over ten thousand. Not unnaturally, the various functions grew in step; in 1963 the central management development department was separated from other personnel activities with a manager and a professional (management development officer). By 1969 there were four professionals together with two personnel research officers; currently there are nine professionals and the research officers. With this increase in strength the department has been able to undertake more ambitious projects.

From the beginning the department has been primarily concerned with

training new managers and monitoring an appraisal and counselling
programme. The researchers' responsibility has been to set up and run
periodic opinion surveys for all employees. More recently training has
been extended to cover all levels of management and the researchers have
become involved in training needs analysis and course evaluation. Possibly
the most significant change in role, however, has been the extension of
training activities from the classroom to the working situation, to internal
consultancy. *MNB*

Managers in ~~IBM~~ are those employees who organise the work of others
for whom they have salary and career responsibilities. It is relevant to
mention that IBM operates a policy of promotion from within. This together
with one of the company's basic beliefs, 'our respect for the individual',
underlines the importance of new-manager training. The parent company
has issued general guidelines for new-manager training which are regarded
as minimum requirements. The training programmes themselves are
developed by IBM UK Limited.

In 1967, outside assistance was involved in running in-company unstructured T-groups. This activity was relatively short lived, however,
and was discontinued following doubts expressed by a number of managers
who had participated. Their reactions showed that the T-groups were not
acceptable to them, possibly because the values developed in the T-group
were alien to those in the company, and were not seen to be helpful.
Subsequent work has been adversely affected by the 'ghosts' of this T-group
experience.

The first significant development resulted from our efforts to find a more
realistic way of training in the skills required for appraisal and counselling
than was offered by role-playing. The outcome was action training, which
attempts to use the experiences and skills of participants within a highly
structured and developmental programme in the context of appraisal and
counselling. Key aspects of the design are that participants are helped to
learn from experience in terms of a systematic approach, and that
managers develop skills by working together on short time-pressured
tasks. Action training was originally seen as a way of developing certain
social skills in individual managers; it has subsequently been used for
helping managers learn about the skills needed for working in groups.

An effort was made to use action training in courses for experienced
managers where the objective was to take them beyond the skills of working
in groups to an understanding of how groups work together within an
organisation. Whereas action training had proved effective in short two-day
designs, it seemed to lose effectiveness over a longer, one-week period.
This led to consideration of other less time-pressured designs for which
ideas were brought together from the various external courses on which
members had participated. The result was an organisation laboratory in
which two groups of 'stranger' managers were taken through the steps of
group development and then given work to do which required the groups to
collaborate.

As this type of training became established, course evaluation began to suggest that all was not well. In reply to the question, 'What have you told your manager about this course?' replies came like 'He should go on a course like this,' or 'He was not interested.' It became apparent that managers were being trained to manage in ways which were resisted by those with whom they worked. Attention then turned to working groups so that they might collectively adopt more effective ways of cooperating. Other experience pointed out the need to integrate this type of group consultancy work with the business life of the group; to work with the group at its normal meetings rather than run special events of a 'training' nature. Training and consultancy activities now take place concurrently.

These, then, have been the steps taken, arising from the need to develop in managers the social skills required for conducting appraisal and counselling interviews with their subordinates, through to learning how to work in groups and organisations, and from there applying these skills in the working environment.

For the future, managers must develop an increased awareness and understanding of the implications of people at work, particularly in a large international company. This should lead to an integrated approach to organisation development which will coordinate training and consultancy activities. While it is difficult to claim validated success for these various activities, it is believed that a positive contribution has been made towards improving the effectiveness of the company in a way which is organisationally acceptable, and achieved on the basis of our own resources (the learning experience accrues to the company rather than to outside consultants). Because the approaches we have used build on one another, achievements are expected to endure and not be seen as gimmicky, flavour-of-the-month techniques.

Perhaps it is appropriate to conclude by commenting on the team of professionals who have developed and directed the activities described here, in terms of their recruitment, background and training. Historically, most of the team have been recruited from outside the company from backgrounds which have usually included managerial training or personnel work; more recently the mix has changed to include internal transfers from personnel, secretarial training and sales. Of the current group of nine, six are graduates but only two have formal social science qualifications. This has meant that most of the current knowledge and skills has been built up during employment with IBM. During induction, most of the team have participated in, then run parts of, the more fundamental courses before taking responsibility for designing and running a course. This knowledge is supplemented by external course work of which Grubb/ Tavistock 'Organisation and Authority' laboratories and Industrial Society 'Action-Centred Leadership' courses are typical. Because of the need for course managers to understand and be committed to their courses, there has always been latitude for them to develop the course design subject to agreement of the colleague with whom they are running the course. This has resulted in personal learning, constant innovation and improvement of courses, while maintaining relative stability of objectives.

The same flexibility has been allowed for in designing and running later organisation laboratories. External training for this has included EIT organisation laboratories, Bath/Tavistock laboratories, the Programme in Organisation Development (sponsored by ICI) and the Leeds University 'Consultancy Skills Laboratory'. The internal laboratories have provided the experience base for consultancy activities, they have allowed the trainer to observe and understand the dynamics of a group doing work, and to assess the impact of his own behaviour when helping the group.

Learning gained through running courses has also been supplemented informally by discussion between members of the group, and by private reading (for which an internal library has been established).

Experience suggests that there is no stereotype for a successful trainer/consultant. Mixed backgrounds, training and career aspirations have provided an open-minded and creative climate for this type of work.

ACTION TRAINING

Action training, as indicated above, was originally developed as a means of helping new managers learn those social skills required for appraising and counselling their subordinates. It was developed because of dissatisfaction with more traditional methods of lecturing which only dealt with knowledge about appraisal, or role-playing which dealt with the skills but in artificial, unreal situations. It was set out, therefore, to create classroom situations in which the managers could be themselves and explore and develop the desired social skills. The approach subsequently used was for developing skills at the group (rather than individual) level to do with leadership and delegation. Other applications include a design for team-building within a work group (organisation development).

This section describes the method adopted and a typical programme. It also reviews other applications of the method.

The method has a number of key features; first, it involves the trainee in a group; second, it deals with behaviour caused by working at a task; third, the tasks are carried out under time pressure which leads to behaviour, such as frustration, curiosity, etc.; and fourth, a systematic approach (including a review) encourages the group to learn by experience.

The course itself usually lasts two or three days (either residential or non-residential), has from twelve to twenty 'stranger' participants and is run by two staff called trainers. There is normally a short half-hour introduction for the entire membership, before splitting into two groups. Thereafter the course remains throughout in two groups. We always stress there is no evaluation or reporting back; this is to reduce risk and to encourage participants to experiment.

The introduction is intended to outline the programme, its purpose, method and timing, and to clarify the role of the trainers. The purpose is expressed in terms of awareness and development of social skills needed for the appraisal and counselling interview; these may be recalled by the mnemonic SLICE — sensitivity, listening, interviewing, counselling and empathy. The method of the course is described by the four key features mentioned above — groups, at tasks, under time pressure and learning by experience. Timing is expressed in terms of start times for the tasks during which special activity times may also be specified. The role of the trainer is described as 'helping the group learn from its experience' — it is essentially a non-directive role placing responsibility for working and learning with the groups.

The programme design is developmental in form. The first tasks are intended to assist individual participants to work as a group, and to develop a systematic approach enabling learning by experience. A task with a tangible product, such as paper decorations, is particularly useful for both these as it allows the group to produce something tangible and measurable. The tasks are typed on slips of paper and handed out at the appropriate times.

TASK 1 (9. 30 - 10. 00) Make paper decorations during a three-minute production run.

TASK 2 (10. 00 - 10. 45) Devise a systematic approach for tackling tasks.

TASK 3 (10. 45 - 11. 45) Make paper decorations during a three-minute production run improving performance over task 1.

Participants work together and set objectives (whatever the criteria — numbers, quality, waste, use of resources) against which they will review their performance. Thus they learn how to learn about working in groups.

TASK 4 (11. 45 - 12. 15) Interview Mr W from the other group to discover how his group organised itself. Counsel him on how his group could be more effective. (You are asked to delegate a member to be Mr W for the other group.)

The main purpose of this task is to give an opportunity to demonstrate interview and counselling skills around a similar experience. This activity with Mr W takes place during a designated twenty minutes. (The exchange of group members is purely a convenience and not intended as in inter-group event.)

TASK 5 (12. 15 - 1. 00) Appraise your group's performance against your improvement plans. Plan further improvements.

This is aimed at consolidating group learning so that, in subsequent tasks, the group may concern itself with the main purpose.

TASK 6   (2. 00 - 2. 45)   Interview Mr X from the other group
                                       to find out his feelings about the
                                       company appraisal and counselling
                                       programme. (Task performance
                                       time 2. 15 - 2. 30)

Implicit in this task is the sensitivity needed to probe feelings and the need for factual information (about Mr X) so that his feelings may be understood, eg, how long he has been with the company, how many appraisal interviews has he had, his performance ratings, etc.

TASK 7   (2. 45 - 3. 45)   Interview Mr Z from the other
                                       group to discover his feelings about
                                       the next appraisal and counselling
                                       interview he expects to have with his
                                       manager. (Task performance time
                                       3. 05 - 3. 25)

TASK 8   (4. 00 - 5. 00)   Counsel Mr Z on how he may benefit
                                       from his next appraisal and counselling
                                       interview with his manager.

TASK 9   (1 hour)   Counsel Mr Y on how he may conduct
                                       a successful interview with his more
                                       difficult subordinate.

These tasks are potentially stressful for Mr X, Y and Z but experience suggests that much learning and helping takes place.

After an overnight break, tasks may be inserted to remind groups of the need to review and to set objectives. The tasks may also remind participants to prepare and plan for the interview situation and not to leave it to chance.

The last task is intended to help participants relate the learning to their own jobs.

LAST TASK (1 hour)   Review what you have learned on this
                                       course and consider how you may use
                                       the learning in your job.

In addition to interview tasks which explicitly require the SLICE skills to be demonstrated, the method of group working implicitly requires the use of the same skills for appraising and counselling between participant and participant, participant and group, trainer and group, etc.

The tasks outlined above relate specifically to the SLICE skills.   The

tasks may be rewritten for other purposes. The initial tasks are also of
value for learning about how a group works; how the group is controlled
either by self-control or by a chairman/manager; they can highlight the need
to clarify the role responsibilities of any differentiated group member -
chairman, observer, scribe, secretary, time-keeper, etc. - and clarify the
norms or habits of the group in terms of decision-making, communicating,
delegating, etc. In this context we have used it for developing leadership
skills in managers, supervisors and project leaders.

Reactions by managers are generally favourable. It is often the first
time that they have become aware of other ways of behaving/managing,
or the way groups work. Some managers see this as an opportunity, others
as a threat. It usually encourages more thought and inquiry.

The team-building (OD) application may be similar to the leadership
design except that participants are the members of a group which exists
in the organisation. The tasks may concern clarification of specific roles
— the group manager, the course director, trainers — and a review of
the management style of the group. Naturally the risk-free environment
of the course cannot be reproduced in this situation; there is a consequent
need for a much higher order of trainer sensitivity. This is a relatively
late development of action training in our own experience and may be
compared with the final section on consultancy. We feel it is most
appropriate for groups working within an autocratic culture where there is
a high dependency on the trainer.

Action training is a training technique aimed at developing in trainees
those specific social skills necessary for working in organisations. It is
characterised by the real human situations which develop and from which
trainees learn by experience and systematic review. The technique gives
the trainer relatively high control through task-setting and timing. The
learning, however, is trainee dependent. Three specific applications have
been outlined: for skills in appraisal and counselling, skills for leadership
and delegation, and skills in real-life team-building.

ORGANISATION LABORATORY

New-manager training in the company has been primarily concerned with
developing skills at individual and group levels (see action training, above).
However, there was a need for managers to have further awareness and
skills in improving relationships between groups in an organisation.
Therefore, a second-stage training design was developed, complementary
to and building upon experience with action training. Following a comprehensive training needs analysis the target population was shifted from
first-line to second/third-line managers (those with managers reporting
to them) as the latter have a coordinating role over the managers and
groups reporting to them. This section describes the training design and
programme developed for this purpose.

The course is designed as an organisation laboratory; it can be regarded as a mini-organisation in its own right; it has a purpose, structure and reality in time, place and membership. It is run as a one-week residential event for up to twenty managers, directed by two professionals, with two or three short visits from senior managers. The purpose of the organisation can be expressed either as 'helping individual managers improve the effectiveness of themselves and their subordinate groups' or to 'enable managers to learn at individual, group and organisational levels'. The second purpose is implicit in the first; managers need awareness at the three levels to improve their effectiveness. The advantage of the first purpose is that it appears job related, is realistic and encourages participants to think about what they have learned on the course in relation to their jobs.

The structure of the course is shown by an organisation chart which shows a management group comprising the two staff members who also double as group trainers, and two work groups comprising participant managers (so divided that they are not in the same group as anyone with whom they work closely). The fact that the staff members have two distinct roles, as course management and as group trainers, gives rise to some confusion in the eyes of participants; this is regarded, however, as a learning opportunity for participants to distinguish the role that course staff are in at different times, and to understand how role may influence behaviour.

The reality of the course organisation lies in its existence for one week at the training centre, with all participants being de facto members. This point seems very important as managers frequently suggest that behaviour on the course is not 'real', 'would not be like this on the job'. There is difficulty in recognising the reality and legitimacy of an organisation which is learning oriented like the course rather than work oriented like the company. The reality of the management role is demonstrated by the instructions given before joining the course, by its programme, and by the fact that catering staff and visitors as well as the participants themselves are doing what 'course management' have decided.

The programme is designed first, to enable development of each of the two groups, then to allow the two groups to interact. Group development is the major concern of the first day and a half; two group interactions are scheduled for the second, third and fourth days leaving the fifth for application of learning to their jobs, and evaluation. Work or formal agenda of the course is set out in the programme and amplified by task sheets which are handed out at the relevant times. The programme design has a different purpose from that of action training: it is less formalised and less time-pressured.

The programme is based on five periods per day (after breakfast, coffee, lunch, tea and after dinner), one of which is left free for relaxation or informal work.

Before the course each participant will have received his joining instructions which advise on administrative particulars including starting-time, location, dress, etc. Also included is a brief statement of course

objectives (as above), a programme and any pre-work. Pre-work is kept
to a minimum; it will usually require the managers to reflect on their
jobs and major difficulties they experience. Managers may be asked, for
example, to complete and return a form headed: 'I could be a more
effective manager if ...' These are collated and used anonymously during
the course.

COURSE PROGRAMME

	Monday	Tuesday	Wednesday	Thursday	Friday
1	(Arrival)	Problem-sharing	Review	Inter-group	Unplanned
2	Introduction Expectations	Planning visitors	Organisational behaviour	Inter-group	Application
3	Role of managers	Planning visitors	Free	Review	Evaluation
4	Decision-making	Visitor 1	Visitor 2	Visitor 3	(Depart)
5	Review	Free	Inter-group	Free	

The course introduction is made by the staff member responsible for the
course. Both groups attend the introduction; this is the only prearranged
time other than 'evaluation' when they assemble together rather than in
their separate syndicate rooms. Administrative matters are covered
before progressing to discuss course background, learning method,
programme and 'role' theory.
    Course background and objectives have been described above. Learning
method is explained as 'learning by experience,' for which purpose review
sessions have been built into the programme. This method places
responsibility for learning with participants rather than with the staff as
with more traditional teaching methods.
    The programme is described as six sessions aimed at group building,
followed by eleven sessions for work between groups, and finally, sessions
for relating the learning to work (application).
    Role theory is expressed in terms of role clarification, role alignment
and role negotiation. For example, so-called 'personality clash' is a
possible indicator of individual/groups working at cross purposes because
of unclear roles. These concepts explain indicators of group effectiveness.
    The role of group trainer is explained as 'helping the group learn from
its own experiences'. The course management role is not referred to at
this stage but is the subject of learning during the second inter-group

event. The staff can, therefore, use their own roles and behaviour as a learning model during the course.

The first five sessions, from 'expectations' through to 'problem-sharing' are intended to encourage group building. 'Expectations', task one, is included so that the group may become aware of what its members expect from the course and to test whether they accord or conflict with the formal course objectives. The task sheet recommends that the group discusses:

'Why you have come here this week.'
'What you understand to be the purpose of the week.'
'What you expect to get out of the course.'
'How you will decide whether the course has been successful.'

This information may be of use later in the week. From the first question it becomes apparent that some members requested to come, others assume it is policy to come. Replies reflect different degrees of commitment to the course which will affect development and effectiveness of the group. Two important indicators for the trainers to notice are: first, whether or how soon members of the new group take time out to introduce one another, which shows the degree of interpersonal awareness. Second, whether the group spends time organising itself for work (chairman/leader, note taker etc.) or starts straight into the task.

The second task, 'role of managers', is intended to assist members introduce themselves to the group by allowing an opportunity to describe their own roles. More importantly it infers that managers at different levels in the company have roles which are different in kind. The task is also highly acceptable as it is company-related. Various ways have been tried to encourage systematic coverage of the topic: 'Discuss your roles as second/third-line managers in the company and highlight how your roles differ from other levels of management.' Alternatively we have used a force field analysis approach in which managers are asked to analyse and discuss those factors helping and hindering them to do their jobs. During this task the trainer will be observing how the group develops formal and informal roles; he may draw the group's attention to this.

The third task, 'decision-making', is a structured exercise intended to make the group aware of the various ways of making group decisions and to examine the appropriateness of these ways. The exercise requires individuals to arrange a list of articles of possible use in a defined situation in priority order; the group then has to agree its priority order. After a period of discussion over priorities the trainer will advise the group of six ways of making decisions (after Schein 1969):

1   By lack of response
2   Authority rule
3   Minority clique
4   Majority vote
5   Consensus
6   Unanimous consent

The trainer can then help the group understand how it has been making decisions on the course and in the exercise so that they may make conscious choices about decision-making. In the exercise, for example, the group may go for unanimity, failing this consensus, and later, when time begins to run out, become more authoritarian.

The fourth task, 'review', is intended as a formal opportunity for the group to reflect upon its development so far and use this information to plan improvements. It may begin by looking again at its decision-making during the previous exercise; it may realise that the authoritarian decisions excluded the contribution of the quieter member who had key information and that this resulted in both a poor decision and lack of commitment of the quiet member. This leads the group to investigate its own member resources more carefully and to test assumptions about 'people speak if they have something to say' or 'if no one says anything we all agree'. This may lead in turn to discussion of the formal and informal roles of group members and the impact of these roles on group effectiveness. Groups frequently experiment with and without leaders; even when a leader has been chosen the group may find it difficult to work with him where his role has not been sufficiently clarified in terms of responsibility and authority. John Adair's three overlapping circles (1968) differentiating task, individual and group-maintenance needs are useful in showing the functions of leadership and helping the group appreciate whether these should be shared or vested in one person.

'Problem-sharing', the fifth task and first on Tuesday morning, is an opportunity for members to clarify difficulties they experience in their jobs. It may be used for amplification of task two, 'role of managers', or for discussing pre-work 'I could be a more effective manager if ...' The task may be described as 'Share with members of your group some of the problems you experience as a manager of managers, noting major differences and similarities.' The trainer will be helping members conceptualise their jobs in terms of role responsibility, authority and relationships as discussed on the Monday. In group terms it assists members to understand one another better; in individual terms it helps build the bridge between work and the course.

The sixth task, 'planning for visitors', is the first of the two inter-group events; it provides an opportunity for the groups to learn about their behaviour as they compete or collaborate in arranging the three sessions attended by senior managers. The groups receive a task sheet: 'You should use the next two sessions for planning the visitors' contributions during the assigned times, so that they may help meet course objectives. Course management has delegated full responsibility for meeting, briefing, introducing and entertaining the visitors to both groups. (Copies of correspondence with the visitors are in the course office.)' The groups are faced with two major decisions: what they want to do with each visitor, and how they will agree this with the other group. It is not unusual for one group to be more task oriented while the other is more relationships oriented; trainers help the groups learn from interaction.

The visitors, who may be directors, will have been briefed beforehand; they expect to be 'used as resources in helping to meet course objectives'. It is important that they are briefed because their role on the course is potentially ambiguous although groups are free to telephone before arrival to check visitors' expectations, preparation, etc. The real value of the visitors' contribution (quite apart from providing a reason for group interaction) is that they are at the centre of company business activities and they have a critical influence on the development of management styles in the company.

'Review' on the Wednesday morning is to ensure that groups learn from the way they collaborated or competed in deciding upon and implementing the agenda for the first visitor. Usually groups related by sending representatives to one another during the course of planning; the trainers encourage the groups to test the role of the representative (is he observer, information-carrier or decision-taker?) so that ambiguity and misunderstanding may be reduced. The trainers will also help by clarifying what work seems to be going on during programme time and what is going on during informal tea/dinner time and why this should be.

The eighth session, 'organisational behaviour', comprises a film about Chris Argyris's view of values and behaviour in organisations; Human Nature and Organisational Reality. It is intended as an introduction to a discussion and analysis of the values to which the group subscribes. Whereas the group can readily explore the way it makes decisions, there are a number of other implicit assumptions which influence group behaviour and effectiveness which are deeper and, perhaps, more difficult to deal with. Openness and trust or the ability to deal with feelings of frustration or uncertainty are typical examples.

The second inter-group event provides an opportunity to apply learning gained from the first inter-group. It also encourages a review of the course so far; 'Plan the use of Friday to ensure that course objectives are met. Your plan should meet the needs of the organisation.' This implies rather more than the first inter-group as it becomes necessary to involve the management group, not only to meet their needs but to check how much authority to arrange the programme they have delegated to the groups. This is usually the first time that the management role has been explored by the groups and it provides considerable material for learning if not for conflict!

'Application' and 'evaluation' are built into the original programme as two course management requirements; the first based on the professional knowledge of management that participants need to relate what they have learned to their jobs; the latter reflecting a management need for feedback so that future courses may be better controlled or designed. Management is prepared to negotiate on time allocation provided these requirements are met.

The programme that eventually emerges for the Friday may vary considerably from course to course. It may be decided to extend the 'review' so that as much as possible may be learned from the inter-group;

time may be spent in groups of various sizes using information generated during the 'problem-sharing' to develop personal improvement plans; management may be asked to make a presentation on the theory behind course design; groups may give personal feedback to their members.

'Application', should it remain in the programme, is normally carried out in triads. The course breaks itself into groups of three managers with similar jobs, the three managers then take it in turns to be client, counsellor and observer. The client requires assistance in relating the learning to his job and developing improvement plans and is helped by the counsellor (helped, in turn, by the observer) who have to demonstrate the appropriate social skills as they help one another.

'Evaluation', the last session of the course, is an attempt to obtain structured feedback about the effectiveness of the course. At this stage it is usually too soon to assess real effectiveness, although participants can indicate their feelings about the course. Evaluation has been in the form of a questionnaire requiring answers to open-ended questions seeking recall of theories (for example, about role), opinions and intentions. The same questionnaire is also sent to the managers some four months later to assess changes modified by experience. Results suggest that there is some relevant learning and application, although a minority of managers remain resistant, if not hostile, to the course and its objectives. Managers may be hostile for a variety of reasons; because they begrudge time away from work; because they are dependent and expect to be told rather than learn for themselves or because they believe the course method is wrong as it regards emoticns and feelings as legitimate subjects for discussion.

The course described has been run along these lines for nearly two years; managers' reactions may be adverse as well as favourable. When the same managers are encountered in consultancy situations they are usually more appreciative and supportive of the consultant. This also suggests that managers may not always be able to use what they have learnt until their job environment (perhaps involving a consultant) changes to allow it.

The course described here appears to be highly structured in terms of tasks for each session. The degree of structure, however, depends on the skill and security of the trainers, and the security needs of the participants. On some courses the trainers have been prepared to change the programme from day three onwards to optimise the learning of their groups. This flexibility is important, but it has to be balanced with the reassurance that structure provides for a number of participants.

The organisation laboratory described here has allowed learning of participants to progress from group to inter-group levels. This training approach provides an opportunity for participants to explore the conceptual issues concerning people working and living in groups and organisations. More significantly, it provides an opportunity for relating these issues to emotional experiences upon which much of their learning is based.

TEAM-BUILDING CONSULTANCY

Manager training, mainly at first-line level has been the major work activity of the central management development department since its inception. With the increase in staffing from four to nine and the skills acquired by the trainers through working on action training and in organisation laboratories, there was a capability and interest in other development work. The nature of new work was indicated by course evaluation forms, answers to which suggested that managers being trained were not encouraged to use their new knowledge or skills back on the job. A number of replies suggested 'my manager should go on this course' or 'he was not interested in the course but told me to clear the backlog on my desk.' It became clear that management development, in the fullest sense of the term, needed to take place outside the classroom within a work context. We have subsequently undertaken a number of activities mainly of a team-building (as distinct from an inter-group) nature. Following this introduction is a general description of an approach and a detailed strategy for team-building consultancy.

The approach as we have developed it, involves a skilled consultant working in a non-directive way with a group of managers who support the consultant's involvement in the context of their normal working meetings. The skills of the consultant are important, although not always recognised by the client groups; he must understand the role he wishes to adopt and be capable of communicating or negotiating this with the group. Negotiation suggests the possibility of a difference in understanding between consultant and group about the consultant's role. This may require resolution by either or both changing their understanding. He should be capable of discussing key indicators of the group's behaviour and helping the group to understand their significance. He must remain acceptable. Having negotiated his role, his behaviour should be an effective mix of support and confrontation. These skills were developed by working with groups in the course environment, by attendance at external organisation laboratories and were further clarified by private reading.

The non-directive character of this approach hinges on the fact that the client group must accept for itself (and not abdicate to the consultant) responsibility for any change or improvement. Additionally, the consultant will only be working with the group for a relatively short period of time; so more effective ways of working must be internalised or fully integrated by the group, if they are to survive his departure.

The reason for working with groups rather than individuals is to overcome the difficulty experienced by managers returning from their courses; any change in the way of working must be allowed if not supported by other members of the group. The group itself must be prepared to support and use the consultant so that his intervention is effective; consequently, it is not appropriate for the consultant to be imposed on the group by higher management.

Involvement by the consultant in <u>working meetings</u> is perhaps one of the more original aspects of the approach. By relating behavioural issues (such as decision-making) to specific work topics, the group can more readily appreciate the relationships between behaviour and work. It overcomes the 'application barrier' often experienced by managers after a course, who may understand the value of, for example, participation, but do not know how to behave more participatively with their colleagues or subordinates. It overcomes the barrier between knowledge and skills. Experience suggests that the consultant will normally intervene relatively little during a meeting except to clarify the purpose of the meeting and really significant occurrences. He will, however, encourage the group to review its achievements and its shortcomings at the end of the meeting. He is helping the group learn by experience.

There are four key parts to establishing a consulting relationship:

1 <u>Discovering</u> and opening discussions with a group of managers who are willing to involve a consultant
2 Clarifying and negotiating the consultant's <u>role</u>
3 Agreeing a <u>contract</u> in terms of situations and timing of work with the group
4 Clarifying <u>objectives</u> that the group might have for the period of consultation

The way in which groups have been discovered has been opportunistic rather than systematic. The company is still in the process of establishing its competence at organisation development and obtaining widespread acceptance of it. Groups have been discovered in an informal way; by talking to a contact, replying to a request for assistance, by working within the personnel function. In all cases an attempt was made to talk to whole groups and to stress the need for, and test, their collective willingness to work with the consultant. In practice, it has not been difficult to obtain agreement from groups to proceed with the consultancy; it has been usual for the senior manager to appear interested and one or two group members to be cynical but not obstructive.

Reasons for groups inviting or allowing the consultant in have varied from the specific to the general, from reason to faith. One group was concerned about attrition of key personnel, another wanted to run a 'get-together'; a third saw management development as being a 'good thing' and wanted more of it; the senior manager of a fourth group felt his operation could be improved but did not know how to do it. Others wanted something better than training.

During the initial discussions it has been usual to clarify how the consultant may see his role. Preliminary discussions may take place with an individual senior manager or with an individual group member before meeting the whole group. The purpose of clarifying role is to enable the group to understand what the consultant will do, and why and how he does it. In addition to helping the consultant, this presents a learning opportunity to the group; the consultant is using his own behaviour as a model both for role clarification and for standard setting.

Presentation of the consultant's role

Role is clarified by presentation to and discussion with the group.   The
presentation is in the form of a prepared handout which comprises about
twelve pages of key words.   It has been typed in this form to allow for
rapid recall — important for managers who have heavy demands on their
time.
    The following paragraphs cover the main pages of the presentation with
explanatory comments.

PAGE 1   Team-building consultancy

                            Background
                            Primary purpose
                            Definition
                            Meetings and interviews
                            Role of consultant
                            Conceptual framework

This sheet is effectively an index of items to be covered in the presentation;
other sheets support the index as necessary

PAGE 2   Primary purpose

                            Improved group effectiveness
                            In work terms
                            In human terms

The purpose of team-building is stated as improved group effectiveness
(of either work or people) whereas group training is aimed at improved
individual skills.   Team-building is structured in terms of roles, agenda
and norms.

PAGE 3   Definition of OD

                            An approach for encouraging exploration
                            and planned development of social pro-
                            cesses in groups/organisations.
                            Social processes:
                              Expectations
                              Norms
                              Decision-taking
                              Communications
                            Planned development (not revolution
                            nor evolution)

'Definition' of OD is very brief. It indicates the importance of behaviour which is not usually seen as a legitimate subject for study.

PAGE 4   Meetings and interviews

> Working meetings :
>   collection of data
>   interpretation of data
> Individual interviews :
>   education of consultant
>   collection of data
> Special meetings :
>   data understanding
>   planning for improvement

'Meetings' explains the three situations in which the consultant will meet the group or its members and the purpose of those meetings. The special meeting is to allow more time to deal with issues than is afforded during working meetings.

PAGE 5   Role of consultant

> Responsible to group
> Data confidential to group
> Non-directive role :
>   helps group collect data
>   helps group understand data
>   helps group use data for improvement
> Helps group to help itself

'Role' emphasises the group's responsibility; it also indicates that the consultant is working for the group as a whole (not for someone else higher up the ladder, or the boss of the group alone) and, therefore, treats subject matter and behaviour as confidential to the group.

PAGE 6   Conceptual framework

> Five levels
> 1 Organisational
> 2 Operational/Task role
> 3 Cultural
> 4 Interpersonal
> 5 Intra-personal

'Conceptual framework' (freely adapted from an article by Roger Harrison 1970) is an attempt to help the group classify and interpret its own behaviour. It implies that group improvement should address the organisation and role levels (1 and 2) which may be the real causes of conflict, before probing the more sensitive and less easily controlled human aspects in the cultural, interpersonal and intra-personal levels (3, 4 and 5). 'Personality clash', for example, is frequently the result of misunderstanding about roles or jobs (at the operational level) rather than fundamental personal antipathy (at the intra-personal level). As suggested above, the consultant's behaviour may be used as a learning model at the operational, cultural and interpersonal levels.

PAGE 6.1   Organisational

                                 (Formal reporting relationships)
Structure related to mission and technology
Based on work-study methods of
     differentiating and re-integrating
Deals with activities and not people

PAGE 6.2   Operational

(To do with the work of groups and
     individuals)
Role :
     responsibilities and objectives
     authority
     relationships
Role clarification
Role alignment
Role negotiation

PAGE 6.3   Cultural

(Concerns how work is done)
Management styles
     Leadership : boss centred or shared
     Decision-making : directive or participative
     Delegation : of responsibility and authority
     Communications : one- or two-way or
         horizontal
     Motivation
     Development of people, or doing work
     Competition or collaboration

PAGE 6.4   Interpersonal

(Group behaviour, extent to which it shows)
Sharing and caring
Openness rather than closedness

Competence with feelings as well as facts
Effect of informal as well as formal roles
Relationships with authority :
  dependent,
  counterdependent or
  interdependent
Power and influence
  concentrated or
  distributed

PAGE 6.5   Intra-personal

                           Behaviour
                           Personality

This last (6.5) is intended to show that, at this fifth level behaviour change
(less talking or agression, for example) may be legitimate business but
personality change is not.

Number of meetings

The contract is agreed in terms of the meetings and interviews which will
take place. Contracts are usually for six to eight meetings, individual
interviews with group members and an optional special meeting. There
appears to be greater opportunity to improve when the normal business
meetings are more frequent — for example, weekly rather than monthly.
A meeting away from usual business pressures is often more effective.
Effectiveness is limited if the group does not have routine, pre-scheduled
meetings; if the meetings themselves are subject to interruption by
comings and goings or telephone calls or if the group operates under
severe time pressure. In these circumstances the special meeting becomes
more critical. The contract is also a means of forcing the group to use the
consultant during the relatively short time he is involved; it allows the
consultant to plan his own time.

Reactions of the participants

Reactions to this type of consultancy seem to vary between groups and
between individuals. Most groups appear supportive and usually acknowledge some changes although they are often unclear about why the changes
have taken place. Typically, it is felt that meetings are improved, simple
decisions are made more easily and quickly, important topics are aired
more fully and often with greater toleration of conflicting opinions.
Agendas are developed by the group rather than left to the boss; individuals
prepare themselves for the meeting and exercise greater self-control.
Many subjects of interest to only two group members are agreed for
discussion outside the meeting. Usually these changes are encouraged by

the senior manager who allows greater individual initiative, also disagreement with him and discussion of his job or his style.

Typical individual reactions reflect anxiety about discussing personalities. Groups seem to cope with this and members become more sensitive and supportive to one another and visiting subordinates.

In spite of the considerable efforts to clarify the consultant's role, the relationship between group and consultant is frequently difficult. Experience suggests that open-ended questions about, say, 'competition' or 'punishing one another' are more acceptable than statements; that the group should only deal with behaviour that has been witnessed by them all; that where individual interviews have yielded relevant opinions, the group should be encouraged to draw these opinions from its members rather than receive them cold from the consultant. Should the consultant miss two or three meetings he may expect re-entry difficulties with the group. The whole relationship issue between the group and the consultant can be regarded as a valid reflection of the group's relationship to authority, and can be used to improve awareness of the group on this subject.

The consultant will inevitably experience some strain due to the relative ambiguity of his role in the group; this will be more acute if he is working within his own department.

Limitations

Limitations of this approach concern the group and its larger company environment; organisational structures and styles of management, for example, may be imposed from without. By discussing these factors, however, the group may be able to clarify its own authority and accommodate itself to the dysfunctional implications of style.

Summary

In summary, the team-building approach described here allows one consultant to assist a working group to review and develop its way of working. This is achieved in the context of working meetings where behaviour is evidently related to the work of the group. In this respect the consultant's activities may be more effective and acceptable, as well as being less time-consuming for the group than other special training activities. Improvements in effectiveness of the group may also, on the basis of an 'open systems' analogy, benefit the larger organisation of which it is a part.

REFERENCES

Adair, John (1968) Training for Leadership (London, Macdonald)
Harrison, Roger (1970) 'Choosing the Depth of Organisational
     Intervention', Journal of Applied Behavioural Science, 6, 181-202
'Human Nature and Organisational Realities'. A BNA film of an
     interview by Saul Gellerman of Chris Argyris.
Schein, E H (1969) Process Consultation : Its Role in Organization
     Development (Reading, Mass., Addison-Wesley)

PART THREE

RESEARCH ON
THE EFFECTIVENESS OF TRAINING

7

The back-home environment and training effectiveness

by David Moscow

One of the main reasons why companies send their managers to T-group laboratories is to give them the opportunity to increase their ability to work and relate effectively with others. But which trainees, in what work circumstances, are likely to benefit from this experience? Do those who have most difficulties in their interpersonal relationships at work gain most, or do those who already have a high degree of interpersonal skill stand to learn more? Then again, when the trainees return to work, which are able to use their training in the job situation? We know that during the T-group the development of a learning climate is crucial. So it would seem reasonable to postulate that the climate and relationships in the trainee's work setting exert some influence on the degree to which he is motivated to try out (transfer) his new learning in the job situation.

This chapter describes an exploratory study in the work setting on the process of change during T-group training and afterwards in the job situation.

A brief review of the technical data and results of the study are followed by a discussion of how the results relate to theories of learning from T-groups. Some case studies from the research illustrate the processes involved, and finally some implications are suggested for managers and training officers wishing to make good use of T-group training.

TECHNICAL DATA FROM THE LEEDS RESEARCH

Subjects

Thirty-one middle and senior managers of British firms who attended T-groups run by Leeds University from 1964 to 1966 were used for the study. Two failed to respond to the final follow-up report forms, and it was not possible to obtain all measures for all trainees. The maximum available number of measures was used in each case, resulting in a sample size ranging from twenty-three to twenty-six.

Criterion measures

Laboratory behaviour change. A system for the content analysis of behaviour was used to construct a measure of the degree of change in each participant's total pattern of behaviour during the T-group. This system was designed by M L Berger and C L Cooper, to whom I am indebted for the use of data collected by them and used here to compile the laboratory behaviour change scores. For details, see Cooper (1968). It was based on trained raters classifying member behaviour from tape-recorded group sessions. Participants' verbal behaviour during T-group sessions was coded into the following eight behaviour categories :

1   Opinions and information
2   Initiating
3   Analysing
4   Supporting
5   Facilitating
6   Defending
7   Expressing
8   Clarifying self, and relieving own tension

Inter-judge reliability was calculated for categories and participants, and most produce moment correlations exceeded 0.80 which is considered an acceptable level of agreement.

Profiles were constructed of each participant's pattern of behaviour early in the laboratory (typically sessions 3, 5 and 7) and late in the laboratory (typically sessions 19, 21 and 23). The first two and the last sessions were omitted, to exclude, as far as possible, atypical behaviour. The measure of overall behaviour change was obtained by summing the percentage shift on each category from early to late sessions.

On-the-job behaviour change. The criterion of behaviour change in the job situation was a 'verified change' score of on-the-job changes perceived by the participant and five to seven of his work associates, six to eight months after the laboratory. This means that the same specific change had to be verified by at least two describers before it was scored. Bunker's system of scoring open-ended report forms into twenty-one behaviour and attitude categories (Bunker 1965) was adopted and satisfactory inter-judge reliability (86%) was obtained.

Factors predicted to influence individual learning during and after training.

1   Perceived relationships with work associates, and
2   Attitudes towards change and training

I interviewed each subject within the three weeks preceding the laboratory. The interviews were semi-structured, covering many aspects of the subject's relationships with his boss, colleagues and subordinates, the most pleasing and worrying aspects of his job, attitudes towards changes in the company and his job, his feelings about attending the laboratory, his perceptions of its relevance to his work and his expectation of change following the course. Great care was taken to establish as good a rapport as possible with the trainee before dealing with the important issues, the interviews lasting an average of two and one-half hours, with some lasting as long as four hours.

Detailed written reports of the interviews were later scored along thirty-four five-point scales by three judges working independently, and inter-judge reliability was adequately high. The items scores of these interviews, plus similar interviews with other managers about to attend T-groups and Grid laboratories were factor analysed and five factors extracted (the items are presented in Figure 7:1):

1   Relationship with boss
2   Relationships with colleagues
3   Relationships with subordinates
4   Awareness of how work associates see him
5   Readiness for change

Work climate.   The trainee's work climate was measured before the laboratory by the participant's boss, and a peer and subordinate with whom he worked closely. The method of measurement was a semantic differential scale. This is a technique developed by Osgood by which ratings are obtained on a number of bi-polar scales; for example, a manager's relationship to his boss could be rated along a continuum from highly trusting to not at all trusting or from highly influential to not at all influential. The rating scales covered perceptions of the work team's autonomy, security, flexibility and openness.

RESULTS

The analysis of the data was rather complex (for details, see Moscow 1969). The significant results can be stated as follows.

FACTOR 1	FACTOR 3

Relationship with boss

Items
Restriction of freedom by boss
Influence over boss
Trust in boss
Support from boss
Encouragement from boss
Openness of boss

FACTOR 2

Relationships with colleagues

Items
Restriction of freedom by colleagues
Influence over colleagues
Trust in colleagues
Support from colleagues
Encouragement from colleagues
Social status (in relation to
colleagues)
Concern over age difference
(in relation to colleagues)

Relationships with subordinates

Items
Restriction of freedom by subordinates
Trust in subordinates
Support from subordinates
Openness of subordinates

FACTOR 4

Awareness of how work associates see him

Items
Awareness of how boss sees him
Awareness of how colleagues see him
Awareness of how subordinates see him

FACTOR 5

Readiness for change

Items
Attitude to change
Attitude to training
Expectation of change following
training
Amount done to facilitate own change/
development
Flexibility

Figure 7:1   Dimensions of interview scores
The dimensions were derived from a factor analysis of rated
questionnaire items

As expected, on-the-job behaviour change was positively correlated with
laboratory behaviour change.   Thus, those participants whose pattern of
behaviour changed most during the T-group also showed most change in
the job situation six months later.   In fact the participants' behaviour
change during the laboratory turned out to be the most important single
factor to influence behaviour change in the job situation.
    Trainees who were moderately aware of how their work associates saw
them before the laboratory showed more change both during the laboratory
and afterwards in the work setting than trainees who were either completely
unaware or very clearly aware.   A post hoc explanation of this finding could

be that where a trainee is clearly aware of how his work associates see him he is likely to get little new feedback during the T-group to disconfirm his picture; at the other end of the scale, where he is completely unaware of how his work associates see him, this may mean that he has rejected cues in the organisation which disconfirm, or contradict, the picture he holds of himself, and will continue to reject them in the T-group.

The trainee's work climate and his perceived relationship with his boss (presumably the most important to him of his work relationships) correlated with laboratory change in the opposite direction to that originally predicted. Thus the more favourable the trainee's work climate and the better his perceived relationship with his boss, the less change he displays during the laboratory. On returning to the job situation, most on-the-job change is found among trainees with only moderately good work climates and relationship with boss.

The trainee's perceived relationships with his colleagues and subordinates did not correlate significantly with either laboratory or on-the-job change. These relationships would generally be less influential on the trainee, and their effect on change may be more difficult to see here because the scores measuring these two relationships involved generalising from the range of separate colleague or subordinate relationships. That is, if a manager had a very good relationship with one colleague and a poor one with another, his overall score would be average.

The trainee's readiness for change showed little relationship to laboratory or on-the-job change. Miles (1965) also found a low correlation between desire for change and on-the-job change, which he felt was due partly to the influence of people saying what they thought they should say rather than what they really felt. This factor may have influenced this result but it seems to me more likely that a generalised desire or readiness for change is less relevant to actual change during and after training than more specific problem-oriented needs (of which the participant may not be fully aware before the training programme).

Figure 7:2 shows how the significant interpersonal factors mediate in the transfer of learning from the T-group to the job situation. The majority of high changers during the laboratory were also moderately aware of how their work associates saw them, had a moderately good relationship with their boss and a moderate work climate and they showed high behaviour change on the job. The majority of low changers during the laboratory had extreme scores on these variables and they showed low behaviour change on the job.

RELATIONSHIP OF RESULTS
TO EXISTING THEORY AND RESEARCH FINDINGS

Some of these findings were unexpected, but let us examine whether they are consistent with other research or theory.

Lewin identified three stages in the process of personal change: unfreezing — changing — refreezing. Unfreezing is a complex process

SITUATION		OUTCOME	
		No. of members showing	
Laboratory behaviour change	Work climate	Low on-the-job change	High on-the-job change
High	Moderate	1	5
High	Extreme	2	3
Low	Moderate	4	2
Low	Extreme	6	0

SITUATION		OUTCOME	
		No. of members showing	
Laboratory behaviour change	Personal relationship with boss	Low on-the-job change	High on-the-job change
High	Moderate	0	4
High	Extreme	3	4
Low	Moderate	5	2
Low	Extreme	5	0

SITUATION		OUTCOME	
	Work climate and relationship with boss combined	No. of members showing	
Laboratory behaviour change		Low on-the-job change	High on-the-job change
High	Moderate	1	5
High	Extreme	3	3
Low	Moderate	4	2
Low	Extreme	5	0

SITUATION		OUTCOME	
	Awareness of how work associates see him	No. of members showing	
Laboratory behaviour change		Low on-the-job change	High on-the-job change
High	Moderate	1	7
High	Extreme	2	1
Low	Moderate	2	1
Low	Extreme	8	1

Figure 7:2 Job situation and course learning related to behaviour change on the job six to nine months after the course

involving the unlearning of old, or habitual attitudes and patterns of behaviour, and the creation of a desire to learn new or modified ones. It is a sort of 'shake-up' process, where familiar things (often taken for granted) are seen in a new light. One's behaviour is revealed as less fixed or certain, and sometimes less effective than it was thought to be. For example, in the T-group, important group processes are intensified and highlighted when some of the usual props to aid group functioning (such as assigned roles) are removed; the sometimes painstaking feedback on the impact of one's own behaviour on the group often provides unexpected revelations, almost like watching a slow-motion film playback of your own golf swing, which at normal speed, and ignoring what happened to the ball, didn't seem to be _so_ different from Gary Player's.

Refreezing is the process of stabilising or 'fixing' the new attitudes or behaviours into the rest of the personality. The new behaviour becomes reinforced when it is confirmed and supported by work associates, and the experimentation and practice proves successful. Following the golf analogy again, it is a little like the process of getting a 'grooved' swing.

Schein and Bennis (1965, p. 276) elaborated on this basic model to suggest the process and conditions for producing attitude and behaviour change during the T-group and afterwards in the job situation, as follows:

> Basically, we are saying that attitude change begins with a (disconfirmation), with some information about a person that leaves him uncomfortable because it is unexpected or violates his image of himself. Often such disconfirming information leaves him feeling anxious or guilty. In order for change to occur, however, some psychological safety must be present in the situation or else the person will simply become defensive and more rigid. Though this process sounds somewhat cognitive, we wish to emphasize the basically emotional features of becoming unfrozen.
>
> If the person comes to feel safe, he will begin to seek some new information about himself which will allow him cognitively to re-define some beliefs about himself or his relationships to others. Such information will be obtained by one of two basic mechanisms: scanning the available interpersonal environment for relevant cues; identifying with some particular other person whose beliefs seem to be more viable.

The trainee, in other words, may begin to try to view himself from the perspective of another person or from the perspective of an array of others. As his perspective, his frame of reference, shifts, he develops new beliefs about himself which, in turn, lead to new feelings and behavioural responses.

> If these new feelings and responses do not fit well with the rest of the person's personality and attitudes and/or if they are not confirmed or reinforced by others, a new cycle of unfreezing and changing is initiated until the person finds attitudes (feelings, beliefs, and responses)

which do fit and which are reinforced.

Schein and Bennis point out that the disconfirmation, which starts the unfreezing process is likely to be more effective where there is a combination of back-home disconfirmation and laboratory forces, than where the process of disconfirmation begins only at the laboratory.

This reasoning is consistent with earlier studies. Mathis (1955) and Stock (1958) suggested that internal conflict has something to do with readiness for learning.

The Leeds study suggests a similar process. The trainees who displayed the most unfreezing of old behaviour patterns and change in their behaviour during the T-group were those who saw themselves as having the most difficulty in their relationships with their boss and who worked in the most inflexible, threatening climates. It seems reasonable to suppose that trainees in such a work situation would feel the most unresolved disconfirmation.

Turning to what happens when the trainee returns home, Schein and Bennis argue that long-run stability of change can occur only when the new attitudes and behaviour patterns are 'relationally refrozen' by their confirmation from people important to the trainee in the organisation. However, the degree to which fade-out occurs if the new attitudes and behaviour are disconfirmed will depend, they suggest, on the degree to which the changes are 'personally refrozen', that is integrated into the rest of the person's attitudes and personality traits.

Again there is support for this reasoning in previous studies. Fleishman, Harris and Burtt (1955) found that foremen's behaviour, following training in human relations (not T-groups) depended more on the leadership style of their boss than on the goals of the training programme. Though this was not a follow-up study of the same group of foremen during and after training, the results suggest that there would be fade-out if trainees changed their attitudes about supervision, then returned to a climate where these new attitudes were disconfirmed.

Sykes (1962), in his study of the effects of a supervisory training course, found that the training led to changes in supervisors' perceptions and expectations of the role of management which the senior management did not share. Despite this the new attitudes did not fade, and the resulting conflict led to increased dissatisfaction and turnover. It seems that these new attitudes were personally refrozen, leading trainees to feel that this company was no longer for them.

Returning to the present study we might expect that trainees who have a very difficult relationship with their boss and a highly conforming and threatening work climate are likely to find that the changes they make during training are either not in line with, or inadequately meet, the expectations of their work associates, particularly their boss.

In Schein and Bennis's terms the changes among these trainees would not be reinforced, and would fade. At the other end of the scale we might also expect that trainees who have a very good relationship with their boss and

a highly autonomous and secure climate would not have much encouragement
to change, either because their previous behaviour was already acceptable,
or because the high degree of autonomy and security at their work provides
others with few opportunities for influencing them. Such trainees may fail
to get confirmation for their changes, and revert to their previous patterns.
Most effective reinforcement and refreezing of laboratory change therefore
probably occurs with trainees whose relationship with their boss is only
moderately good and whose work climate is not extreme in autonomy,
security, flexibility and openness. The findings in this study support this
reasoning. Trainees with moderate relationships with boss and moderate
work climate show most on-the-job change.

SOME CASE STUDIES

Looking at all the data in a more clinical fashion the process described
above became very apparent; a few examples might help to show this.

1   Mr A worked in a very insecure and guarded climate. Resignation had
recently been forced on a senior member of the management team, of which
he was one. He did not trust his boss an inch, since his boss interfered
with his work to the extent of 'ruining the situation' for him, and had not
discussed any policy matters with him regarding his job for three years.
He felt that he received no encouragement or support and saw no point in
disagreeing with his boss since his boss 'must win'.
    Mr A's boss and colleagues found him difficult to work with, rather
suspicious and either petulant or withdrawing from conflict. During the
T-group the trainers reported that Mr A had a deep emotional experience.
This report was consistent with his high behaviour change score during the
laboratory, the changes he perceived in himself, and his enthusiastic
reports to his colleagues on returning home from the course.
    However, eight months later when the report forms were received it
appeared that, though Mr A was seen as a little more cooperative and able
to discuss matters more reasonably, the change still did not satisfy some
of his work associates. His boss felt that Mr A had changed for the better
initially, but had recently regressed to his former attitudes and behaviour
during the pressure of a company takeover. Mr A himself reported that
he felt his learnings were long-term, and was unable to use them in his
present difficult situation, because his boss's behaviour 'prevented
reasonable discussion.'.

2   Mr B had a similarly difficult though less extreme relationship with
his boss and worked in a very inflexible and conforming climate. He was
a young thirty-year-old graduate who was being sent to the training course
'to learn to deal with junior management, foremen and workers, on their
own level'. At the laboratory, Mr B had a high change score, and was
rated by the trainers as having gained a lot.

Back in the job situation there was a general agreement that he had changed his entire outlook. His foremen were pleased about his new tolerance and understanding towards them, but thought it bad for discipline when he used the same approach to workers. His boss and colleagues were also ambivalent about the change : 'Mr B has changed from a vigorous, brash young man to an immature psychologist,' commented a fellow manager.

Mr B was aware that some people regarded his present outlook as bad for discipline, but he persisted in this approach. The new attitudes and behaviour were obviously personally refrozen and, as in the Sykes study, he left the company within a year after the training course.

3   Mr C and Mr D both worked in climates characterised by a very high degree of freedom and security. Neither worked closely with his boss. Mr C was head of his regional sales office, and expecting an early move through promotion. He regarded the course as part of his reward for good work, was keen to learn, but felt he had no particular interpersonal problems to deal with. He showed medium change during the laboratory, but none in the job situation.

Mr D in charge of a specialist engineering function, was very free to run his section with little pressure from outside. On returning from the course he was seen to be more open to others' views, began involving subordinates more, and passed on more information. Some of these changes gradually faded. One subordinate remarked that receiving the follow-up form had the effect of switching Mr D on again, and information once more started to be passed on.

4   Mr E had a moderately good relationship with his boss, and an average work climate. His boss thought of him as a first-class engineer, but inconsiderate of his colleague's views, and needing to see himself as others see him. He showed high change during the laboratory, and returned to his job more aware of the impact on others of his previous dogmatic and individualistic approach. Cooperation between functions at his level were regarded by his boss and colleagues as vitally important, so Mr E, who was seen as more cooperative and a better team man, had his new behaviour strongly reinforced.

IMPLICATIONS FOR THE ORGANISATION

Much of the interpretation of the findings in this chapter is post hoc and based on a small number of subjects. However, the results seem to be consistent with previous research, and can be interpreted within the framework of one model, that of Schein and Bennis (1965). Taking the two together some implications for the manager or training officer involved in the recruitment and selection of members of the organisation for T-group training become clear. (Let us assume for this discussion that the organisation's main objective in sending a delegate is to help him improve his own competence in dealing with people — thus we leave aside here such cases as the organisation sending a delegate merely to report back on the value of the course for others in the organisation.)

This study suggests that transfer of learning from T-groups to the job situation is most effective when the learning is congruent with, or relevant to, the rest of the trainee's current personal or interpersonal needs. Though the trainee may be keen to learn, it would seem that he is only motivated to change his responses to an observable degree if he sees a specific need for change. Hence, ethical reasons apart, we can see why, in the selection process, unwilling members should not be dragooned into a T-group, however much it is felt they might 'need it'. Such persons are less likely to unfreeze and experiment with new behaviours during the T-group laboratory, and, as we have noted, behaviour change during the T-group was our best predictor of long-term transfer to the job situation. The chances of successful learning for these people (and for the T-groups in which they participate) will be greater if they are made aware of the areas where their interpersonal skills are not up to the demands of their current or future position, and, through feedback and support from within the organisation, can come themselves to the point of wishing to do something about it.

At the other end of the scale it seems likely that little change can be expected in a trainee who regards himself as already very effective interpersonally and sees the course as merely a reward for good service or as a mark of prestige. Rewarding employees in this way is all well and good, but then we should not expect to see immediate and obvious gains. Greater long-term value is likely to accrue if the trainee is helped by his boss, before the course, to see areas in which he may learn and possibilities for applying his learning when he returns.

One man I interviewed in this study (a sales manager in a large international company) was under the impression that his selection for the 'latest management course', was a reward and a portent of 'higher things'. He was, in the event, both disappointed and threatened by the nature of the course, and complained to his boss that these courses were a complete waste of time for the company. His boss later confided to us that Mr X was a problem: he often rubbed clients up the wrong way and he did not know it. He had hoped that Mr X might have learnt this during the course and would find out how to do something about it. Perhaps Mr X's boss predicted that if he had told him the real reason for his selection he might have been less willing to go, and that all that was needed was to ensure that he got there ... when he would be 'taught'.

Admittedly assessing training needs and selecting the right participants is not easy, but when trainees return from the course support and confirmation must also not be forgotten. It is confusing and disheartening to the trainee to be told 'learn a lot, but don't think that you can bring in all those new-fangled ideas here!' Too little trust, support and freedom to experiment in the back-home situation — especially from the boss — will inhibit transfer. On the other hand, conditions of very high trust, support and autonomy before the course are not likely to create the disconfirmation needed to start the unfreezing process — after all, in such conditions who wants to change?

We can see, then, that the best value out of T-group training cannot be obtained if it is regarded as an isolated event, unaffected by the conditions prevailing within the organisation. Careful observation can help the manager or training officer choose the best divisions, department or individuals where training should begin, and also the timing of it. The need for this careful preparation is, I feel, already being recognised by many training officers, but how often does this pre-planning go to waste through the training officer feeling that once the course is arranged he has no further responsibility and can only keep his fingers crossed that something from the course 'sticks'? The learning process involves an interaction between the individual, his T-group, and the organisation.

REFERENCES

Bunker, D R (1965) 'Individual applications of laboratory training', Journal of Applied Behavioural Science, 1, 131-48.

Cooper, C L (1968) 'A study of the role of staff trainer in human relations training groups', unpublished PhD thesis submitted to University of Leeds.

Fleishman, E A, Harris, E F and Burtt, H E (1955) Leadership and Supervision in Industry (Bureau of Educational Research, Monographs number 33) (Columbus, Ohio State University).

Mathis, A G (1955) 'Development and validation of a trainability index for laboratory training groups', unpublished PhD thesis, University of Chicago (see T-group Theory and Laboratory Method, ed. L P Bradford, J R Gibb & K D Benne (New York, Wiley, 1964), chapter 15).

Miles, M B (1965) 'Changes during and following laboratory training: a clinical-experimental study', Journal of Applied Behavioural Science, 1, 215-42.

Moscow, D (1969) 'The influence of interpersonal variables on the transfer of learning from T-groups to the job situation', in Proceedings of the Sixteenth International Congress of Applied Psychology (Amsterdam, Swets & Zeitlinger).

Schein, E H & Bennis, W G (1965) Personal and Organization Change through Group Methods: the Laboratory Approach (New York, Wiley).

Stock, D (1958) 'Factors associated with change in self-percept', in D Stock and H A Thelen, Emotional Dynamics and Group Culture (New York University Press).

Sykes, A J M (1962) 'The effect of a supervisory training course in changing supervisors' perceptions and expectations of the role of management', Human Relations, 15, 227-43.

This chapter is based on a paper read at the XVIth International Congress of Applied Psychology, Amsterdam, 18-22 August 1968. (See Moscow 1969.)

8

The outcome of a group training course for Ford Motor Credit Company

by Pamela Berger

This chapter is a report of research carried out on a one-week group dynamics course in Ford Motor Credit Company Limited. It is based entirely upon questionnaires, administered to the course participants, their boss and one subordinate at the time of the course and again six months later.

In November 1968 a group dynamics course was held for thirteen branch managers. The goals of the course were as follows:

1   To develop in course members a greater awareness of their behaviour, the behaviour of others, and an understanding of the impact of this behaviour; and to relate this to problems of communication and leadership
2   To demonstrate some of the problems involved in overcoming resistance to change and in opening up communication in work groups and to experiment with ways of breaking down some of these barriers to communicating
3   To improve personal skills of listening and communicating

The course was four and one-half days, held at a residential training centre. Mornings were devoted to exercises which pinpointed problems of cooperation and conflict between individuals and groups, decision-making and power relationships. The afternoons and evenings were devoted to sensitivity training, free discussion and short lectures providing theory of individual and group behaviour. For three days the after-lunch sessions were free time in which members played games, talked informally or rested.

THE PROJECT

Management expressed interest in an evaluation of the effectiveness of the course and I was called in to do this. I was not connected with the running of the course so that an unbiased view could be maintained.

Learning was expected in three areas:

1   Increased skills of communication and awareness of group processes
2   Increased effectiveness in leadership and decision-making in groups
3   Increased effectiveness of working relationships

In order to assess whether the course met its goals, several questionnaires were given to course members, their bosses, and their subordinates, at the beginning and end of the course, and six months after its conclusion. From the responses to these questionnaires, changes in performance and in work climate were assessed.

Individual course member learning was assessed in two ways:

1   By comparing the analysis of a case study focusing on problem-solving skills done at the beginning and end of the course and six months later

2   By asking course members if they had changed over the six-month period and in what way

Verification of job performance change was possible by asking bosses and subordinates if the course member had changed and in what way.

Effects of the course on the organisation were assessed

1   By asking course members and work associates what difficulties and problems they experienced on the job. Differences in the kinds of problems reported before the course were compared with those reported six months later

2   By asking bosses and subordinates to characterise the managerial attitudes and work climate within the organisation

Again, change in work climate was ascertained by comparing questionnaires completed before the course with those obtained six months later.

Figure 8:1 shows the times at which questionnaires were given to the groups and the number of questionnaires returned. 'B' refers to the beginning of the course, 'E' refers to the end of the course and 'F' refers to the follow-up six months after the course.

NAME OF QUESTIONNAIRE

	Case study	Participant change questionnaire	Organisational climate	Job problems
Questionnaire given to eleven course members	B E F	F	—	B F
Number returned	11 8 7	7	—	11 7
Questionnaire given to fifteen work associates	—	F	B F	B F
Number returned	—	12	15 14	15 14

B = before course
E = end of course
F = six months after the course

Figure 8:1   Number of questionnaires returned

DESCRIPTION AND RESULTS OF QUESTIONNAIRES

Case study

'Bomber raid over the Ruhr' (Gil and Bennis 1968) was designed to stimulate thought about human behaviour leading to the diagnosis of a problem concerned with group norms and behaviour, strategy of social change, social influence and power. The case also posed problems of immediate corrective action.

The following instructions were given with respect to the case:

If you were allowed to ask five questions, what information would you wish to get? From whom? Please rank the questions in order of importance. How do you explain the situation as described? What action would you take if you were the squadron commander?'

Responses were scored according to five categories by two raters working independently of each other and without knowledge of which point in time (B, E or F) the responses were made. The responses were scored in the following categories.

Diagnostic skill

1 Managerial style — responses were analysed in terms of being consistent with McGregor's classification of management style. The characteristics of Theory X are that management's role is to direct and control the behaviour of others to fit the needs of the organisation. Without this control people are passive and resistant to change and to organisational needs.
   The relevant characteristic of Theory Y is that management's role is to structure the organisation so that people can achieve personal goals by working towards organisational goals. This implies that people are not passive and are by nature motivated to do a good job.

2 How thorough and broad was the manager's analysis of the problem? Was it based on one explanation rigidly held to and on superficial observations or was it based on explanatory themes, recognising several causes with possibilities of re-evaluation?

Action skills

3 How much understanding and consideration does the respondent show of short-term as against long-term solutions in his recommendations for action? Are the recommendations narrow, concentrating on one part of the system independently of other parts and aimed at solving only the immediate crisis or are they dealing with several problem areas, recognising the interaction between sub-systems and holding promise for realising long-term improvements?

4 Facing or avoiding problems. Does the respondent avoid the problem (by seeking more information, ignoring relevant data) or does the respondent seek to cope with the problem and its underlying causes?

5 Management style — action recommendations. Are the action steps consistent with a Theory X or a Theory Y managerial style?

Results

It was found that by the end of the course there were substantial increases in both action and diagnostic skills (Figure 8:2).

	Begin N = 9	End N = 8	6 months later N = 7	Meaning of Scores
A Diagnostic skill				
1 Theory X <u>v</u> Theory Y analyses	3	2.75	2.5	1 = extreme Theory X 7 = extreme Theory Y
2 How thorough and broad is the analysis?	2.12	3.62*	3.37	1 = superficial level of analysis 10 = very thorough level of analysis
B Action skill				
3 How much understanding and consideration of short-term <u>v</u> long-term solutions is conveyed?	2.5	3.62*	2.25	1 = narrow understanding and short-term actions 10 = great understanding and long-term actions
4 Facing up to or avoiding problems	4	5.25	5	1 = not facing up to problems 10 = facing problems
5 Theory X <u>v</u> Theory Y action recommendations	2.25	3.75	1.5	1 = action based on Theory X 10 = action based on Theory Y

Figure 8:2   Course members' average scores in five categories of analysis of case study

Starred numbers indicate a statistically significant change from beginning-of-course scores, that is, the change is significant in the statistical sense - there is a very low probability that a change has occurred through chance (p = 0.10)

Managers analysed problems more broadly, saw solutions with more understanding of long-term consequences, and advocated action which faced the problem more. The management style of diagnosing problems was unchanged but the management style of taking action was more consistent with Theory Y management. Six months later, although many changes had diminished, the diagnosis of the case study was still more thorough and broad than at the beginning of the course.

PARTICIPANT CHANGE QUESTIONNAIRE

This was given to course members and work associates six months after the course. Course members were asked whether they had changed their behaviour in working with people in any specific ways since November 1968, as compared to the previous year and if so, to describe these changes. The boss and one subordinate of each course member were asked the same question about the course member with whom they had contact. Responses to this question were placed into categories developed by Bunker (1965). Examples of categories where change was most frequently reported include the following:

1   Relational facility: more cooperative and tactful, less irritating, easier to deal with, able to negotiate
2   Increased interdependence: encourages participation more, involves others, greater leeway to subordinates, less dominating, lets others think
3   Self-confidence: increased assurance
4   Insight into self and role: understands job demands better, more aware of own behaviour, better adjusted to job

Result

Of the seven course members who responded, six felt that they had changed. Bosses of course members felt that five of twelve had changed and subordinates felt that five of nine course members had changed. Only one respondent reported change to be negative in nature. Five questionnaires were not returned and four people refused explicitly to complete them. Figure 8:3 presents the categories of change into which responses were placed if they were mentioned more than once. Examples of responses to the change questionnaire are presented in Figure 8:4.

Conclusion

Half of the course members were seen by work associates as having changed from the time of the course to six months later. These changes related predominantly to improved work relationships, to greater self-insight and to more self-confidence. These findings are consistent with

CATEGORY	NUMBER OF RESPONSES
A Behaviour changes	
Increased interdependence	8
Relational facility	6
Functional flexibility	3
Risk-taking	2
Sending and receiving communication	2
B Attitude changes	
Insight into self and role	4
Self-confidence	3
Awareness of human behaviour	2
Sensitivity to others' feelings	2
Acceptance of other people	2

Figure 8:3   Number of responses placed in each of the categories of course members' change as reported by course members and their work associates
Number of returned questionnaires : Course members 7, bosses 3, subordinates 9

MEMBER REPORTS OF SELF CHANGE

'I consider that I have improved in my 'listening' to both colleagues and subordinates and arrive at the necessary decision with more information and alacrity than before.'

'I am much more appreciative of the fact that to communicate effectively one has to try very much harder and realise and understand the other man's problems.'

'I more readily discuss problems pertaining to my work with my subordinates.'

'Far more inclined to consider the effect of my actions on other people.'

'I do not feel I have changed my behaviour ro any great degree.'

REPORTS OF MEMBER CHANGE BY WORK ASSOCIATES

'He has gained a good deal of assurance in his manner and dealings with other people, especially with those for whom he is responsible.'

'His confidence has improved and extends itself to those around him.'

'He has shown a greater tendency to lead rather than push.'

'He has developed a tendency to look upon those in authority as sometimes being stupid and therefore ignores or is slow to carry out their directions.'

Figure 8:4   Examples of responses to change questionnaire

those where subordinates reported less work problems with management above them six months after the course (see problem census, Figure 8:5). Thus some course members were noticeably able to improve work relationships. The fact that almost all course members who completed the questionnaire felt they had changed and this change was not always verified by work associates may be due to work associates failing to notice changes; course members being over-optimistic about their learning; or course members changing in relationship to work associates other than those who completed the forms.

Organisational climate questionnaire

This was given to work associates at the beginning and six months after the course to assess the impact of the course on work environment. This questionnaire comprises ten statements of opinions and is designed to assess the managerial attitudes perceived to be held by people in the organisation. The individual is asked to decide whether the people he has contact with would agree, have no opinion or would disagree. Opinions focused on the following areas : degree of participation in decision-making; ways of dealing with barriers to communication; and flexibility of procedure.

Results

It was assumed that if course members learned from the course then changes in the climate should be detectable by work associates.
   Of the ten statements of opinion, four revealed considerable changes, they were as follows :

1   'Meetings should be used to communicate information rather than to
     solve problems'
Ten of fourteen respondents changed their assessments of organisational opinion. The changes were not systematic, however, some people reported less agreement six months later. This would indicate that people changed their views about the purpose of meetings but in differing ways.

2   'Decisions should only be made after everyone's ideas have been
     heard'
Eight of fourteen respondents changed their assessment of organisational opinion, seven towards greater agreement. This would indicate that there was a greater concern with participative management six months after the course.

3   'You should discourage others from telling someone if they have a
     grievance against him'
Nine of fourteen respondents changed their assessments; most tended to change toward greater disagreement. This would indicate a greater

degree of openness and desire to resolve problems of communication and human relations.

4   'A man should be promoted on the basis of his actual performance
       rather than his potential'
Nine of fourteen respondents changed their assessments;   slightly more than half changed toward greater agreement.

Conclusion

Several changes in organisational climate were found. The first three of these changes are in line with the goals of the course which aimed at dealing with problems of communication, leadership and decision-making. The last change does not appear to be related directly to the course and may be the result of other organisational factors. One can infer that these opinion changes are reflected in behavioural changes as well — that is, not only were attitudes about decision-making and meetings changed six months later, but decisions and meetings were in fact different. A much more detailed study involving interviews and direct observation of meetings would be needed to confirm this conjecture.

Problem census

This was given to course members and work associates at the beginning of the course and six months later to ascertain what impact the course had upon the work environment. This questionnaire asked the respondent:

1   To describe any recurring problems, difficulties and dislikes about
       the job
2   To discuss whether there were barriers to communication between
       people, where and why they occurred

Results and conclusions

In order to compare before and after frequencies of problems, the average number of problems mentioned per person (that is, number of times problem mentioned divided by number of respondents) was calculated. These are shown in Figure 8:5. Six months after the course, course members reported more problems with management, company policy, and slightly more problems with colleagues than at the beginning of the course. These upward-oriented problems may be new ones which are the result of trying new approaches or taking more initiative within the company. The new problems related to lack of desired authority, the inflexibility of the system and lack of understanding of their problems by others.
     Subordinates of course members reported fewer problems with management, company policy and with subordinates six months after the course.

PROBLEM AREA	Course members		Subordinates		Bosses	
	Begin N = 11	6 months later N = 7	Begin N = 12	6 months later N = 11	Begin N = 3	6 months later N = 3
Relationship with management, my boss	0. 6*	1. 3	0. 7	0. 2	1. 0	0. 7
General atmosphere	0. 3	—	0. 2	0. 2	—	—
Company policy	0. 5	1. 3	0. 7	0. 3	0. 7	0. 7
Nature of work	1. 1	0. 9	1. 5	1. 1	1. 3	1. 0
Colleagues	0. 1	0. 3	0. 1	0. 1	—	—
Clients	0. 2	0. 1	0. 3	0. 2	—	—
Subordinates	0. 4	0. 4	0. 2	0. 1	—	—
Personal	0. 5	0. 7	0. 2	0. 3	—	—

* Average problems per person = $0.6 = \frac{7}{11} = \frac{\text{total number of responses}}{\text{number of respondents}}$

Figure 8:5 Average number of problems per person by management level reported at the beginning of the course and six months later

For example, problems of communication upwards decreased in frequency from five to one. This finding was consistent with the changes reported regarding organisation climate — for example, more freedom to express grievances and more participative decision-making. Bosses of course members reported the same frequency of problems both before and after the course. This was not surprising as they were likely to have had less contact with course members than subordinates had with course members.

SUMMARY

This evaluation describes an example of management training provided to one level of management. That the course achieved its goals is borne out by the increased member skills of diagnosing behavioural problems and formulating relevant action. This was corroborated on-the-job by bosses and subordinates six months after the course. They reported that half of the members changed in such areas as increased insight, self-confidence, ability to relate to others and interdependence.

The most interesting specific finding was that course members themselves reported a greater frequency of problems with management and with company policy while, on the other hand, subordinates of course members reported fewer problems with management and company policy and in addition reported several changes in organisational climate (such as more participative decision-making and more openness in expressing grievances). It would appear that course members had successfully improved their work relationship with subordinates but had encountered more difficulties upward. This could be related to increased confidence, to seeing the job in a wider perspective, or to being more in touch with the problems of their subordinates. This result is consistent with several other evaluation studies which found that implementation of course learning often meets resistance from within the organisation, especially where other members have not attended a similar course. The amount of change possible from course members depends on both course learning and on an organisational climate which is supportive of the learning (Fleishman 1953, Miles 1965, Moscow 1969). One solution to this problem is to introduce training at as high a managerial level as possible. Another is to hold multi-level courses for individuals who relate to one another on the job (team training).

It is interesting to note that the management orientation (Theory X or Theory Y) of course members changed little. This would indicate that members learned skills (such as communicating openly and facing problems directly) rather than changing their basic style of management. It was also found that the amount of learning decreased from the end of the course to six months later. These conclusions were later found to be consistent with the observations of one of the top managers in the company.

The fact that some managers did not show job performance change is probably due in part to resistance to change within the organisation and in part to lack of learning from the course. Similar types of courses, but of two-week duration have reported change rates of 65 to 80 per cent (Bunker 1965, Moscow 1969, Miles 1965). By comparison, a change rate of about 50 per cent for a one-week course is considered adequate.

GENERAL COMMENTS ABOUT THE PROJECT

It is noted that only seven out of thirteen questionnaires were returned by course members. This lack of return limits the confidence one may place in the results in that it is not known whether those who did not respond had similar opinions to those who did respond.

Some caution is necessary in relying on findings from questionnaires, especially when obtained through the post. The respondent's motivation to complete the forms may affect the results. For example:

1   The amount of time spent on the questionnaire would be affected by
    work load, and other pressures
2   The attitude towards the research may be positive or negative and
    motivations to spend time filling in questionnaires may be high or low
    accordingly
3   The attitude towards the researchers may be one of trust, seeing
    them as objective and impartial, or one of wariness, seeing them as
    an extension of management

The number of unreturned questionnaires was high for a project of this size.
It may have been helpful in this regard for the researchers to have had some
face-to-face contact with respondents. It appeared that commitment to the
research was moderate at the beginning of the course and was reduced six
months later. This may be understood as a normal reluctance to fill in
forms; however, I feel that there was suspicion throughout the life of the
project which influenced the choice of forms employed and the number of
questionnaires returned.

REFERENCES

Bunker, D R (1965) 'Individual application of laboratory training',
   Journal of Applied Behavioural Science, 1, 131-48
Fleishman, E A (1953) 'Leadership climate, human relations training,
   and supervisory behaviour', Personnel Psychology, 6, 205-22.
Gil, P & Bennis, W G (1968) 'Science and management : two cultures?'
   Journal of Applied Behavioural Science, 1, 75-108.
Miles, M B (1965) 'Changes during and following laboratory training :
   a clinical experimental study', Journal of Applied Behavioural
   Science, 1, 215-43.
Moscow, D (1969) 'The influence of interpersonal variables on the transfer
   of learning from T-groups to the job situation', in Proceedings of the
   Sixteenth International Congress of Applied Psychology (Amsterdam,
   Swets & Zeitlinger). (See also Chapter 7.)

A more detailed version of this report (Working Paper number 7), including
copies of the questionnaires used, can be obtained from North London
Polytechnic, Management Department, Camden Town, London NW1.

9

Selection and training effectiveness

by Mel Berger

The question of who should attend a group training course is often raised.
'There is a manager in my department who can't get along with his
colleagues, should I send him on a T-group to get him sorted out?' 'Mr
X is an outstanding manager, should we let him know how much the company
values him by sending him on a high-priced course?' 'How can I select
the individuals who are likely to benefit from group training?'
   The answer is all too often based on intuition, expediency, or hope.
Sometimes, someone with expertise in group training is consulted. But
even in this case the reply is most likely to be based on the personal,
recalled experience of a few trainers. Although this is better than un-
informed intuition, there is usually a lack of factual verification.
   At one extreme, Fraser (1965) suggests that 'the only people who should
be allowed to take part in a T-group are those who don't really need the
experience. Those who would benefit greatly from the experience ought
not to be allowed in.' On the other hand, Miles (1965) believes 'that a wide
variety of personality types can profit from laboratory training.' This
chapter will consider selection with an aim to proposing understandable
and realistic criteria, based on available facts and upon practical
experience. Most of the pertinent research has been carried out on
managers attending 'stranger' T-groups. As such the chapter will be
directed at selection for T-groups, although the discussion applies to other
group-training approaches as well.
   Before starting, it should be pointed out that evidence based on system-

atically collected information is sparse. On the other hand, several individual research studies do suggest promising avenues of approach to the problem.

INDIVIDUAL AND ORGANISATIONAL SUITABILITY

The problem of selection can be looked at from two viewpoints, that of organisational suitability and that of individual suitability. For example, an individual might be likely to benefit from the T-group but the application of his learning may be hindered by organisational pressures. People in this situation often report positive changes in non-work, social or marriage, relationships but not on the job. In the extreme case they may be so frustrated by the lack of organisational support that they leave the company. Similarly, the organisation may be open to change but a given individual may not be.

The question of organisational suitability, or relevance, is dealt with in depth in Chapter 7. It is worth emphasising here that any training carried out without consideration of the organisation's goals or a management development context runs the risk of being irrelevant to the organisation. The organisation should begin by clarifying goals, for itself and for its members, and then decide how best to meet these goals. Thus it can be assessed whether group training is appropriate. For example, T-group goals, such as sensitivity, diagnostic and action skills, are most appropriate where organisational procedures are not rigid and where open communication is essential. It has been my experience that individuals from organisations which are extremely hierarchical and mechanistic (such as hospitals and the Army) are likely to learn less from a T-group and to apply less of the learning to their job than individuals from more flexible, participative organisations. A more structured, task-oriented form of group training is generally more appropriate for the former organisations. The more similar the organisation and the training method, the more likely the individual is to see the training as relevant to his job and the more likely it is that the organisation will accept the changes in the trainee's behaviour.

This chapter is primarily concerned with assessing T-group suitability from the point of view of the potential T-group participant. Two questions are considered:

1   Are there some individuals who should not attend T-groups?
2   Which individuals are likely to learn most from the T-group and which are likely to learn very little?

ARE THERE PEOPLE WHO SHOULD NOT ATTEND T-GROUPS?

A useful set of criteria for an industrial manager or training officer, is proposed by Beckhard (1965).

The T-group is inappropriate as a learning device if the goal of the student and/or his boss or the institute to which the student (participant) belongs is primarily one of the following:

1 To deal with a 'sick' person or one who cannot be handled within the organisation
2 To convert the student to a new way of life
3 To institute a rapid change in personality and/or behaviour
4 To try to produce a maverick — one with 'new ideas' — in a hostile back-home culture

These criteria suggest that the organisation should not expect that a training course, in itself, will solve their problems by changing people overnight. A source of possible confusion in the criteria is in the use of the word 'sick'. This seemingly applies to the individual who is not coping with his job very well. It could be that he is merely in the wrong job or it could be that he has difficulty in coping with most demanding situations in life. The latter sort of person could be a risk to send on a T-group. By risk it is meant that he is unlikely to gain from the experience and that he may find it upsetting. The T-group can be likened to a new job, a job quite different from one's previous job or to taking an important examination. The experience will contain uncertainties, ambiguities and demands but most individuals are able to learn and grow from this. For an individual who has severe difficulties in coping with demanding situations and uncertainty, the T-group is not appropriate. This person's solution may be a less stressful, more stable job or perhaps psychotherapy.

Although T-group critics always raise the danger of mental breakdown, the possibility of this happening is slight indeed. It has never happened in my personal experience of training approximately fifty groups. Further, based on discussions with numerous other trainers, I have heard of only two instances of breakdowns out of approximately 300 groups and 3000 participants. This frequency is about that found in most situations in life. Lubin and Zuckerman (1970) found that 'T-group stress at the highest point of emotional arousal is of the order of that experienced by college students just prior to an examination.'

This is not to deny that breakdowns are a possible danger. Several factors, however, considerably reduce the risk of breakdowns. An experienced trainer can usually assess when a group member is having difficulty in coping with the situation and can act to ameliorate it (by such things as providing help and protection in the group, personal counselling outside the group, or recommending the person not to continue on the course). Other group members can usually sense this as well and often provide support to the individual. Further, individuals generally know their own limits and involve themselves in any situation only to the extent they feel it is safe and likely to be rewarding.

WHICH PEOPLE WILL LEARN MOST FROM T-GROUPS?

Although selecting out 'problem' individuals is critical, it is not likely to apply to more than a few potential candidates. What about the majority of 'normal' people; is it possible to predict which of these are likely to learn most from a T-group? In order to fully explore this question let us consider how people learn in T-groups. The clearest statement of this is by Harrison (1965) who suggests a four-step process.

1   The individual initially deals with the T-group situation by presenting himself in a manner which is somewhat typical of his usual response to group situations, to authority and to other group members

2   This behaviour meets with moderate failure or a negative reaction by others

3   Learning occurs through a process of confrontation of one's own behaviour and perception with alternative behaviour and perceptions of others. 'The individual may explore alternatives to his current orientations . . . . Thus, we see persons who are initially active, responding to failure by withdrawal (and) dependent persons may rebel' (p. 410).   However, 'if almost all members of a group share a common framework for dealing with some important class of interpersonal phenomena (for example, power and authority), then they will not provide the confrontation which leads to exploration . . . and consequent learning' (p. 299). On the other hand, too much confrontation may lead people to withdraw from the situation rather than to explore and learn from it.

4   The individual finds support in the group to experiment with alternative behaviour patterns and to see the relevance of the group experience to himself as a person. If this is not the case the person may conform overtly without really learning.

It is not implied that all people react to the T-group in this manner, rather that this is the process whereby learning occurs. Thus, if an individual does not react in a typical way (perhaps he did not want to attend the course or he is unsure why the company sent him and therefore is reluctant to get involved) then he is unlikely to learn. Similarly, he may react typically in the group but not be confronted by other group members in which case he is again unlikely to learn very much.

Let us return to the original question now of which individuals are likely to learn most from a T-group experience. Three studies, including a recent one by the author, will be considered in order to find some answers to this question.

A study by Harrison and Lubin (1965) considered participants from the point of view of their style of relating to people. They assessed the manner in which people described other people and characterised each group member by whether he was more concerned with people or more concerned with tasks (or work). They found that person-oriented T-group participants functioned more effectively but learned less than did task-oriented participants. They explain that 'task-oriented participants thus appear to have been more strongly confronted, challenged, and pushed toward change by their training experience' (p. 293). This result challenges Fraser's viewpoint by suggesting that those who would benefit greatly from a T-group, do so! Unfortunately, information about whether there was subsequent behaviour change on the job was not obtained. This information is critical, of course, in assessing whether changes during training represent adaption to a particular situation or represent more lasting learning.

The most comprehensive T-group study was conducted by Miles (1965) who examined whether certain participants would be more able than others to adapt and use the T-group situation for learning. He found that group members who were high in flexibility and high in need for affiliation were seen by themselves and by trainers as learning more than members who were low in the two characteristics. However, these differences were not related to behaviour change on the job. Miles concluded that 'a wide range of personality types can profit from laboratory training' (p. 221). It would appear then, that individuals of varying personal styles of adapting to groups can benefit equally from the T-group.

Democratic and autocratic styles

Following Harrison, I approached the question of 'who learns most' from the viewpoint of which members were most likely to be confronted and challenged by a T-group experience (Berger 1972). Although confrontation need not lead to change, it was reasoned that it is an important precondition to change. Group member values or ideology were assessed along a continuum from 'democratic, participative, Theory Y' on the one hand to 'autocratic, traditional, Theory X' on the other hand. As the T-group approach to learning is based on participative values — that is, group members are encouraged to take responsibility for their own learning and are not directed by the trainer to pursue a given task, it was assumed that members with autocratic values, being more confronted, would learn most from the course. This was tested on seven management courses run by Leeds University Department of Management. Four of the courses were of two weeks duration and three were of one week.

A method for categorising behaviour was developed and used by raters (not involved in the group itself) listening to tape-recorded group sessions. Some behaviours were assumed to be those encouraged by T-group trainers (this assumption is supported by a previous study of trainer behaviour by Psathas and Hardert, 1966) as they were consistent with T-group goals : expressing feelings, supporting other members, analysing group behaviour and giving feedback (these are termed participative behaviours). Other behaviours were probably not encouraged, such as asking for and providing information, and defending oneself. By comparing behaviour ratings for each individual obtained at the beginning and again near the end of the group, behaviour change scores were calculated for all participants; thirty-six from two-week groups and twenty-four from one-week groups. A measure of behaviour change on the job, based on one devised by Bunker, was obtained about six months after the course by asking the trainee's work associates whether or not the trainee had changed. The data were collected from twenty-five participants attending the two-week courses and nine attending the one-week courses. With a sample size of only nine, any conclusions drawn pertaining to change on the job from one-week groups should be considered highly tentative.

Participative behaviour in the T-group

The first part of this study considers the extent to which behaviour in the T-group was participative. It was found that T-group trainers' behaviour was frequently participative throughout the life of the group (about 55 per cent of their total behaviour). Members' behaviour, on the other hand, was seldom participative at the beginning of the group (about 18 per cent) but became increasingly so by the end of the course (about 36 per cent).

Thus the T-group leads to member behaviour change in the direction of becoming more participative in the majority of cases.

Of thirty-six members of two-week groups, twenty-one increased their frequency of participative behaviour by 10 per cent, while fourteen showed relatively no change, and one decreased his frequency of participative behaviours more than 10 per cent. Of twenty-four members of one-week groups, eighteen increased their frequency of participative behaviours by 10 per cent or more, five showed little change, and one decreased his frequency of participative behaviours by more than 10 per cent.

Among those members who increased participative behaviours over the length of the group, the specific type of change varied: some becoming more supportive, others becoming more expressive, while still others tended to be more analytic.

Management style and participation

The second part of the study explored the performance of different types of members. It was found that democratic members functioned more effectively — that is, they behaved more participatively — throughout the group than did autocratic members.

It was then discovered that the more autocratic members showed most behaviour change from two- but not one-week groups. In one-week groups both autocratic and democratic members changed similarly. The measure of behaviour change on the job yielded parallel though more striking results. Those with autocratic values, and who attended two-week groups, showed more change on the job than those with democratic values (though the differences were not quite significant in the statistical sense). In one-week groups, the findings were reversed, democratic members showed change while autocratic members showed no change. Comparing members of one-week groups with those of two-week groups, it was found that democratic members of two-week groups changed only slightly more than democratic members of one-week groups. Autocratic members of two-week groups, on the other hand, showed very high change whereas autocratic members of one-week groups showed almost no change (see Figure 9:1).

Personal characteristics	Two-week groups behaviour change on the job			One-week groups behaviour change on the job		
	Low	Medium	High	Low	Medium	High
Democratic members	4 (22%)	9 (50%)	5 (28%)	1 (25%)	3 (75%)	0
Autocratic members	1 (13%)	2 (25%)	5 (63%)	4 (100%)	0	0

Figure 9:1 Details of the relationship between personal characteristics and subsequent change on the job
Of group members with participative values attending two-week groups, 4 (or 22 per cent) showed low change, 9 (or 50 per cent) showed medium change, and so on. Personal characteristics were assessed from the Christie version of the F scale (Christie, et al. 1958). The types of on-the-job changes frequently reported were such things as, 'more cooperative and tactful', 'encourages participation more, involves others', 'greater self-confidence' and 'less dogmatic and arbitrary' (categories from Bunker 1965).

This suggests that individuals whose values are autocratic need more time to gain maximal long-term benefit from the group than democratic individuals. Members of both one- and two-week groups showed similar amounts of behaviour change during the course but those attending two-week courses showed more subsequent change on the job than those attending one-week courses. This is possibly because one week was not time enough for people to sufficiently practise what they had learned.

APPLICATION OF COURSE LEARNING

To sum up these three studies, it would appear that some characteristics of course members lead to course learning but have a neutral effect with regard to learning applied to the job. Flexibility and need for affiliation are examples of these. It seems likely that people who are highly flexible and high in the need for affiliation adapt to the demands upon them in a given situation. Thus, they adapt to the T-group, but then re-adapt to their own job when the group is over, without being able to make any changes (perhaps because they are too flexible and not persistent enough).

Other characteristics (such as having autocratic values) are associated with both course learning and changes on the job. When individuals with autocratic, non-T-group values attend a T-group they are likely to be confronted and challenged on basic issues, but given sufficient time (two weeks), much of the learning which has occurred is likely to remain after the experience is over.

GUIDELINES FOR SELECTING T-GROUP MEMBERS

The T-group is a training method which generally places emphasis on open communication and a democratic, participative style of relating and working as a group. People who normally behave in this fashion and who value this approach adapt relatively easily to the situation and are likely to be able to use it to learn. However, as they already have a fairly high level of competence in skills which the T-group emphasises, they potentially have less to learn from the situation than individuals who are generally more autocratic in their approach to people and groups.

This is more obvious when seen by analogy. If you take tennis lessons and are already a reasonably good tennis player you are likely to improve your game but not as much as someone who is not such a good player prior to the lessons. On the other hand, you are likely to refine and reinforce your skills.

Thus, the _more_ autocratic manager has a greater potential for learning, though it will take him longer to do so. But, given two weeks, it is likely that he can learn skills which can be applied to his job.

This leads to the conclusion that most people, regardless of their initial skills in dealing with people, can benefit from T-group training.

The following guidelines are proposed to aid participant selection. Again it must be stressed that more research needs to be done to verify and refine the few thorough studies which have been conducted to date. Though very time consuming and requiring cooperation from organisations sending people on these courses, this research is essential if management training of all types is to be improved.

1   Those individuals who are most autocratic are likely to benefit from a two-week course much more than from a one-week course
2   Those individuals who are most democratic are likely to learn slightly more from a two- than a one-week course
3   Those individuals who have difficulty in coping with non-routine job demands and new situations, are unlikely to learn from a T-group. Although the risk of breakdown is very slight, these people may reduce the level of learning for other members

Identification of those individuals who are most and least likely to learn from the T-group is best done by a sensitive manager or training officer, preferably one who has had experience of T-groups. Selection interviews may also be helpful in providing the individual with information about the course. If information about the nature of the course and what the individual probable that candidates who are unlikely to benefit from the experience will choose not to go. It seems clear that the application of course learning to choose not to go. It seems clear that the application of course learning to the job is not straightforward : people need a sufficiently lengthy course and a facilitative job climate. Where there is doubt about the suitability of a potential candidate it is best for the organisation to discuss the matter with the people doing the training. In this case it is likely that they will interview the man himself.

A final word of caution, lest all democratic managers are sent to one-week courses and autocratic managers are sent to two-week courses. Several research studies (Harrison 1965 and Smith 1970) suggest that optimum learning results from a mix of individuals with different personal styles and ways of perceiving the world. Thus, although autocratic individuals learn more than democratic individuals in two-week groups, it is doubtful that they would learn as much without some democratic members to confront them and to help them learn. Indeed, the only way that individuals with differing styles can learn to work with one another is to have contact with one another. To be able to understand and to accept differences in others is important learning in any training situation.

In conclusion, it is suggested that organisations make decisions about appropriate types of training based on the organisation's objectives and the expected learning of the type of training in question. With respect to the training course itself, the following are important :

1   Careful preparation of a participant by the organisation in terms of the aims of his attending the course will promote a positive motivation to learn from the course

2   Careful thought about which type and length of course is appropriate for a given individual will increase the likelihood of the individual learning from the course

3   Sufficient support in the organisation when the manager returns from the course will facilitate the transfer of learning from the course to the job setting

REFERENCES

Beckhard, R (1965) 'The appropriate use of T-groups in organisations', in T-Group Training : Group Dynamics in Management Education, ed. G Whitaker (Oxford, Basil Blackwell).

Berger, M L (1972) 'Participant personality and behaviour in training groups', unpublished thesis to be submitted to the University of Sussex.

Bunker, D (1965) 'Individual application of laboratory training', Journal of Applied Behavioural Science, 1, 131-48

Christie, R et al (1958) 'Is the F scale irreversible?' Journal of Abnormal and Social Psychology, 45, 171-99.

Fraser, J M (1965) 'Some misgivings about T-groups', in T-group Training : Group Dynamics in Management Education, ed. G Whitaker (Oxford, Basil Blackwell).

Harrison, R (1965) 'Group composition models for laboratory design', Journal of Applied Behavioural Science, 1, 409-32.

Harrison, R & Lubin, B (1965) 'Personal style, group composition and learning', Journal of Applied Behavioural Science, 1, 286-301.

Lubin, B & Zuckerman, M (1969) 'Level of emotional arousal in laboratory training', Journal of Applied Behavioural Science, 5, 483-90.

Miles, M B (1965) 'Changes during and following laboratory training : a clinical-experimental study', Journal of Applied Behavioural Science, 1, 215-42.

Psathas, G & Hardert, R (1966) 'Trainer interventions and normative patterns in the T-group ', Journal of Applied Behavioural Science, 2, 149-70.

Smith, P B (1970) 'Trainer styles and group composition', SSRC Annual Report, 1970.

PART FOUR

THE TRAINER

10

The group leader
and training effectiveness

by Cary L Cooper

Much evidence (Campbell & Dunnette 1968, Cooper & Mangham 1971) is
available to support the use of the T-group as a highly important training
method. Very little is known, however, about how or why it is effective.
There is a great need for a better understanding of how the T-group works
and the trainer's contribution to its success.

The trainer's task is to draw attention to individual and interpersonal
behaviour as it develops within the group. In a book concerned with T-group
training, <u>T-group Theory and the Laboratory Method</u>, Blake (1964) has
suggested that the primary task of the trainer in a T-group is one of
creating the most productive climate in which 'the participant can accept
responsibility for his own development and can develop valid communications with others.'

Tannenbaum, Weschler and Massarik (1961) suggest that to facilitate this
the trainer can perform several broad functions in the group. First, he
can initiate points for discussion and exploration. For example, he may
focus attention on his role of authority figure or use research instruments
in structuring particular situations for potentially useful insights. Second,
he can establish a model of behaviour in the group. He may encourage and

accept criticism, express his own feelings, or direct feedback to other people. And finally, he can facilitate the flow of communication by initiating, clarifying and encouraging the discussion of essential issues such as those of leadership, group avoidance of task work, interpersonal conflict and intimacy.

Most people involved in T-group training have some idea about what makes an effective or ineffective trainer in a group. And, as Bolman (1968) has suggested, more often than not these notions are highly intuitive and have not been systematically investigated. The aim of this chapter is to look at the trainer's role in light of research evidence.

RESEARCH ON TRAINER INFLUENCE AND PARTICIPANT CHANGE

Some progress has been made in relating the trainer's personal needs to his behaviour in the group (Deutsch, Pepitone & Zander 1948, Reisel 1959), in assessing his effect on the perceptions of participants (Lohmann, Zenger & Weschler 1959, Vansina 1961), and in drawing attention to his impact on the development of the group (Stermerding 1961, Psathas & Hardert 1966, Mann 1961). Although these studies, in one form or another, demonstrate the effect of the trainer in the T-group environment, none of them states in what form this influence exists and how this relates to participant learning. That is, how or by what process does he influence these outcomes? If we are to use research to help us in practical decisions on organising T-group training, no study can escape the obligation to be clear about the conditions necessary to establish a connection between the trainer and the results of his influence on individual change. As Harrison (1966) emphasises, 'Hopefully, we shall soon have instruments which will permit us to assess trainer style and relate it to the kind and extent of outcomes.' Some research of this kind has recently been undertaken.

Identifying with the trainer

Peters (1966) examined the relationship between trainer identification and personal change. He found that participants who identified with the trainer, as assessed by direct, indirect and projective measures, showed personal learning within the T-group. In respect to trainer identification, the participants' perception of self converged with their perception of the trainer and the trainer's perception of self. This convergence was noted for most participants in six two-week T-groups. The same results were not obtained in the control group. In addition, it was discovered that identification and personal change were stronger for men than for women and for participants with similar occupational backgrounds to the trainer. Peters's interpretation was that 'for identification to lead to personal change in the T-group may require a model (trainer) whose attitudes, values and behaviour are relevant, functional and realistically attainable for the person.' That is, the trainer must be relatively similar to the trainee for identification to take place.

The study, although interesting, has several shortcomings. It assesses personal change by reference to trainer ratings and peer ratings at the end of the group. This has two disadvantages : first, a measurement is made only after the event that was supposed to have induced change; and second, neither of these measures of 'change' has been validated unequivocally. In addition, the control group used by Peters differs markedly from the trained group. The former consisted of graduate students in their early twenties, while the latter consisted of high-status middle-aged administrators (business, school, nursing, government and public administration officials). It would have been better to have used a control group more similar in age and occupation. Nonetheless this study is interesting in that it attempts to link participant change directly to the trainer and to indicate that identification may be a relevant learning mechanism in T-groups.

Self-disclosure by the trainer

Culbert (1968) investigated the effects of trainers disclosing information about themselves to members of two student T-groups. The same trainers participated in both groups. They were provided with 'job descriptions' which set forth guidelines for their behaviour in each group. These descriptions called for the trainers to behave similarly in both groups — that is, to differ only on the experimental condition of being more self-disclosing in one group and less self-disclosing in the other. The first part of the study substantiates that the 'job descriptions' could be successfully carried out. The trainers were judged as more self-disclosing in the more self-disclosing condition than in the less self-disclosing condition by each of three separate measures. The second part of the study found that the members of the less self-disclosing group more often perceived their relationships with the trainers and a specified partner as facilitating interpersonal learning. Those in the more self-disclosing groups more frequently viewed their relationships with the rest of the group as facilitating interpersonal learning.

As Culbert points out, interpretation as to the desirability of this difference is not clear. It could be argued that the members of the more self-disclosing group have learned to create better relationships free from dependence on the trainer. Alternatively, it could be argued that participants in the less self-disclosing group, by being centrally involved with the trainer or specific partner, were participating in qualitatively richer relationships than members of the more self-disclosing group.

Further, participants of the more self-disclosing group had a significantly higher degree of self-awareness than those of the less self-disclosing group, a difference which narrowed with time. Culbert concludes from this that the participants of the more self-disclosing group appear to have modelled their participation after their self-disclosing trainers (participants followed the trainer's example). This explanation, Culbert notes, is given further support from clinical impressions reported by the two trainers and the group observer.

In his conclusion, Culbert argues strongly that there is an optimum level of self-awareness for T-group participation and that early attainment of this level is to the group's advantage. It follows from this that self-disclosing trainer participation is called for at least during early meetings. Upon attainment of this self-awareness level the trainer need not be as self-disclosing. It is to be noted, however, that much of this conclusion is speculative in view of the small sample size.

Empathy

Bolman (1968) added to Culbert's approach in investigating the relationship among certain dimensions of trainer behaviour (similar to self-disclosure) and member learning. He found that one dimension of trainer behaviour was crucial in the learning process, the dimension labelled congruence-empathy. It was found that where the trainer had a close match between his feelings and his behaviour in a given situation (genuineness or congruence) and was empathic there was more participant learning. While the data in this study were limited, in that they were based only on the perceptions of the group members, it does support the evidence in other social influence situations (Rogers 1957, Barrett-Lennard 1962) that change agents who are seen as congruent or honest provide opportunities for individual learning.

Social influence

Cooper (1968) investigated Kelman's (1961) theory of social influence with respect to the trainer in T-groups. He focused on two processes of social influence : identification and internalisation. It was proposed that the participants' perception of the trainer's characteristics will determine which process of social influence is likely to result and, consequently, the way in which participants will change. He found that when the influence process was based on identification with the trainer (that is, when the trainer was seen to be attractive):

1   The participants became more like the trainer in their attitudes and in their behaviour
2   Changes in the participants' self-concept did not occur
3   The participants' work associates did not report them as having significantly changed six to nine months after the T-group

When the influence process was based on internalisation (that is, when the trainer was seen to be congruent or genuine):

1   Changes occurred in the participants' self-concept — for example, change towards an increased match between perception of himself (self-percept) and of how he would like to be — self-percept and other

participants' perception of him, and self-percept and actual behaviour
2   Participants did not become like the trainer in their attitudes and
      behaviour
3   The participants' work associates reported them as having changed
      six to nine months after the T-group

It is important to note some of the assumptions implicit in this study.
First, it was assumed that attractiveness and congruence are mutually
exclusive dimensions; this, on the surface at least, may not be the case.
Second, it was assumed that it is the participants' perception of the
trainer's behaviour and not the trainer's actual behaviour that is the primary
basis of influence in the relationship.

More fundamentally, an assumption throughout this paper has been that
the trainer is the principal source of influence. At the same time, we
must consider whether factors other than the trainer (such as group composition, group format, and intra-group dynamics) may be determinants of
participant change. In future research we must examine each of these
factors by introducing them into analysis and investigating how the relationship between trainer behaviour and participant change is affected by them.

It cannot be claimed that any of the above studies have exhausted all
aspects of trainer influence. However, they do reach interesting and
practical conclusions, and are provocative of further research.

IMPLICATIONS OF THE RESEARCH

If one accepts that a main concern of the T-group is to create a learning
environment where change is transferable to situations beyond it, then the
studies reviewed above may have some useful applications. First, the
results of two of the studies (those by Peters and Cooper) suggest that
individuals who participate in an identification-based influence process prefer
a learning strategy that emphasises the trainer. Although modelling after
the trainer may help the individual initially to cope with the ambiguous
training situation, it may also create, in some participants, an unnecessarily high level of dependence on him that is not likely to lead to the
transfer of learning to the back-home environment. To deal effectively
with this possibility the trainer and participant must feel free to explore
the nature of their relationship. The trainer can help the participant in
this respect by calling attention to the participant's behaviour in the group
which may reflect identification. Identification may appear in the form of
members imitating the trainer's behaviour or being the 'ideal T-group
participant'. Since the individual is displaying 'appropriate' group behaviour
and since the trainer may be over-concerned about the success of the group,
particularly in the earlier sessions, he may be reluctant to highlight this
individual. Attention must, however, be drawn to this behaviour as a
'spring-board to get away from him (the trainer) as the sole criterion for
effective behaviour and look to themselves and one another as important

resource people' (Argyris 1966).

Second, most of the above studies (Culbert, Bolman and Cooper) found a strong relationship between participant change and whether the trainer was perceived as being trustworthy, self-disclosing, and genuine with group members. That is, when the trainer was seen to behave in a way that did not mask his true feelings, participants changed in desirable ways. This is very important in the learning environment of a T-group. As Smith (1969) suggests, 'a trainer who shows himself worthy of trust will help to develop a climate of internalisation in the group.' Emphasis must therefore be placed on this aspect of trainer style in the selection and training of trainers.

Third, the research points to the desirability of training the trainer to emphasise participants' responsibility for their own learning. Each trainer behaves in ways that create conditions for both psychological success and failure, which is related to their own needs and psychological make-up (Argyris 1966). The trainer can exploit his role in the pursuance of his own needs, particularly in his desire to be liked or to exercise power. As Schein and Bennis (1965) emphasise, 'the possibilities for unconscious gratification in the change-agent's role are enormous and because of their consequences (for the health of the client as well as the change-agent) they must be examined.' It is essential that training programmes be developed that focus on the trainer's motives and how these may enable or prevent the participant from learning in his own way.

Thus, the trainer's influence on the group is considerable. It is important for him to have a high degree of awareness of himself and his impact on others. This can only be obtained through extensive experience in groups where he receives feedback and has the opportunity to try different behavioural approaches.

Although these studies deal with T-group trainers, the conclusions are also of relevance to other types of trainers, teachers and counsellors. Within broad limits set by the group's general level of ability and compatibility, any trainer or teacher has a wide scope of potential influence on the group in which he is the authority.

REFERENCES

Argyris, C (1966) Exploration and Issues in Laboratory Education (Washington DC National Training Laboratory).

Barrett-Lennard, G T (1962) 'Dimensions of therapist response as causal factors in therapeutic change', Psychological Monographs, 74, number 42.

Blake, R R (1964) 'Studying group action', in T-group Theory and Laboratory Method, ed. Bradford, L P, Gibb, J R and Benne, K D (New York, Wiley).

Bolman, L G (1968) 'The effects of variations in educator behaviour on the learning process in laboratory human relations education', unpublished PhD thesis, Yale University.

Campbell, J P & Dunnette, M D (1968) 'Effectiveness of T-group experiences in managerial training and development', Psychological Bulletin, 70, 73-104.

Cooper, C L (1968) 'Study of the role of the staff trainer in human relations training groups', unpublished PhD thesis, University of Leeds.

Cooper, C L & Mangham, I L (Eds) (1971) T-Groups : A Survey of Research (New York, Wiley).

Culbert, S A (1968) 'Trainer self-disclosure and member growth in two T-groups', Journal of Applied Behavioural Science, 4, 47-74

Deutsch, M, Pepitone, A & Zander, A (1948) 'Leadership in the small group', Journal of Social Issues, 4, 31-40.

Harrison, R (1966) A Conceptual Framework for Laboratory Training, (Washington DC, National Training Laboratory)

Kelman, H C (1961) 'Processes of opinion change', Public Opinion Quarterly, 25, 57-78.

Lohmann, K, Zenger, J H & Weschler, I R (1959) 'Some perceptual changes during sensitivity training', Journal of Educational Research, 53, 28-31.

Mann, R D (1961) 'The development of the member-trainer relations in self-analytic groups', Human Relations, 19, 84-117.

Peters, D R (1966) 'Identification and personal change in laboratory training groups ', unpublished PhD thesis, Alfred P Sloan School of Management, MIT.

Psathas, G & Hardert, R (1966) 'Trainer interventions and normative patterns in the T-groups', Journal of Applied Behavioural Science, 2, 149-70.

Reisel, J (1959) 'The trainer role in human relations training', paper read at the Western Psychological Association meeting, April 1959.

Rogers, C R (1957) 'The necessary and sufficient conditions of therapeutic personality change', Journal of Consulting Psychology, 21, 95-103

Schein, E H & Bennis W G (1965) Personal and Organization Change through Group Methods : The Laboratory Approach (New York, Wiley).

Smith, P B (1969) Improving Skills in Working with People : the T-Group (London, HMSO)

Stermerding, A H (1961) 'Evaluation research in the field of sensitivity training', unpublished manuscript, Leiden, Netherlands Institute of Preventive Medicine.

Tannenbaum, R, Weschler, I R & Massarik, R (1961) <u>Leadership and Organization</u> (New York, McGraw-Hill).

Vansina, L (1961) 'Research concerning the influence of the T-group method on the formation of the participants' social values and opinions', in <u>Evaluation of Supervisory and Management Training Methods</u> (Paris, Organisation for Economic Co-operation and Development).

11

A course for training trainers

by Alan Beardon

Group dynamics training is rapidly becoming a regular feature of modern management and other training programmes. Active participation of trainees while they are working together is becoming the focus of many learning situations. In this way the skills of decision-making, gaining commitment to decisions, of planning and communicating within and between groups are being learned by personal involvement in situations which demand the exercise of these skills. It seems that many training designers are beginning to give up not only the 'tell and sell' teaching methods but also role playing and case studies. In their place a whole range of participative training techniques is growing up. In these, the key to improved performances through training is seen as the individual manager's willingness to study his own personal style of working. And the key to creating a learning climate within which such a study can fruitfully be made is the skilled trainer.

Unfortunately the rising awareness of these training needs has not yet been followed by a systematic training for those trainers who might meet them. There is a shortage of trained personnel. Until recently there has been no centre where training in the participative techniques of group dynamics could be attained. Those who had not been able to travel to the USA or Holland have mostly acquired their skills by contact with those who had. Many have developed themselves as trainers simply by doing the job and learning from the hits and misses of their experience. At long last, a few systematic efforts to train trainers have emerged. One of these programmes is described below. It illustrates how a training course was planned and carried out including the types of exercises used in the overall design.

The Management Department of North London Polytechnic ran its first course aimed at trainer development in December 1969. The aim was to develop the skills of group dynamics trainers and others who have the opportunity of using group dynamics in their jobs. As advertised, the course was to include :

1   An initial intensive T-group, including a critical examination of the trainer's role and the effect of his interventions on the group
2   Seminars and demonstrations on the role of the trainer within the organisation, diagnosing of training needs, and consulting with ongoing task groups
3   Seminars pertaining to the diagnosis of group problems, group training theory, and the role of the trainer
4   Practical work on the design of courses and the types of exercises which are available

Participants were mostly senior industrial managers, training officers from the Civil Service and industry, and teachers.

PLANNING THE COURSE

There were twenty-five participants in the programme, and five staff members, four of whom were full-time staff of the North London Polytechnic and the other a consultant with experience of trainer development programmes in the USA and Europe. A minority of participants had not previously attended a full-length T-group and for these it was thought necessary to provide this experience in the first week. For others the priority was to learn about trainer intervention strategies and course planning. It was hoped to introduce course members to a wide variety of group dynamics techniques, many of them developed at the Polytechnic over the past few years.

On Monday of the second week, the staff had committed the participants to planning and running a 'real-life' one-day training seminar on communications for a group of thirty-six graduate secretarial students attending the Management Department's eighteen-week intensive course. It was thought that this experience would provide an important source of learning about course design and implementation.

Other planning considerations included the facts that participants had a wide range of experience which would be useful to tap, and that many had expressed a wish to be personally counselled on their trainer potential and style and the steps they could take after the course to further their own development as trainers. There were sixteen men and nine women attending the course. A video tape machine was available on certain days.

A questionnaire sent out before the course provided the course staff with information about members' previous experience, together with their individual aims and expectations. Aims included

> To gain greater competence in training in-company courses
> To find out if group dynamics can be applied to my job
> To increase my action skills for running groups
> To see different approaches that a trainer can take
> To learn new teaching skills
> To learn theory and principles of course design
> To get feedback on my personal style
> To learn about planning and evaluating training activities
> To learn about intergroup theory and skills
> To develop sensitivity skills for intervening in work groups within my organisation

These questionnaire responses were used to guide the staff in planning detailed activities.

THE FIRST WEEK

The first week's activities consisted of a regular mix of the following elements : T-groups, task groups and group dynamics exercises.

T-group

Twenty-five participants were divided into three groups based on previous T-group experience. About twice as many hours were allocated to the relatively inexperienced group during the first week. The goals of the T-group were to create a learning climate, to learn about diagnosing group processes, and to obtain feedback about the impact of the trainees on one another.

A video recording was made of the inexperienced group during the opening of the Monday T-group session and another of the Friday morning session. Both sessions were played back on Friday afternoon to the group for the purpose of observing itself in action and comparing changes or lack of them over the course of the week. It was noted, for example, that although group members were more open with one another on Friday, the same type of group pressures to conform to group standards was in evidence. The observation led the group to question and later to modify the way it worked.

As is common, learning in the T-group varied widely according to the preference of and decisions by the group members and trainers. One group wanted to concentrate on giving personal feedback for a time, another on its processes of decision-making. My own group spent a large amount of its time early on studying the norms that had developed within the group.

What should be done when one member refused to introduce himself in an acceptable way? Had not the rest of us given background information about our careers, schooling and family? Why should he not want to? This led to a lengthy discussion in which the group became aware of difficulties involved in becoming an accepted member of the group. How much do and should group members have to conform to group standards in order to be accepted? Only by dealing with such issues could a level of trust be attained where genuine relationships and communications could be made. Over time facades of politeness were discarded. We came to welcome frank expression of feelings and personal information about one another in the group. Members questioned assumptions and early impressions of one another. They learned about how to help one another and that it was not always as easy as wanting to help. People found resources of understanding and support that they had not suspected. They experimented with methods of more 'open', sometimes non-verbal, communication.

In the other two T-groups, learning included insights, sensitivity and the development of action skills in the following areas:

1   Different styles of individual influence and their effects on others
2   Problems of facilitating contributions of all group members
3   Gaining insights into what behaviour helps and what behaviour hinders building trust between group members
4   Handling conflict, involvement and withdrawal in groups
5   Coping with feelings involved in working in a group of men and women

Task groups

Members of the two more experienced T-groups were allocated to one of three task groups according to their job background. Thus one task group was composed of training officers, another of industrial managers, and another of individuals interested in becoming T-group trainers. All task groups had the job of planning and running a one-day seminar for a group of twelve graduate secretarial students. Each group had one staff member whose brief was to be a consultant to the group. The goal of the task group was to provide a real training situation from which trainees considered the problems involved in planning the course and designing exercises.

It was thought very important to make a clear distinction between the work of the T-groups, aimed at personal learning through discussion of its own processes and experience, and the task group, aimed at getting a job done. Unlike the T-group, the task groups had a deadline to meet, hence there was a constant time pressure: a plan had to be devised, agreed and implemented.

Before planning the one-day course, task group members interviewed their prospective trainees in order to diagnose what the secretaries wanted to learn. In order to explore the sort of exercises that were possible, they commonly brainstormed ideas and visited the inexperienced group who were doing specific structured exercises. Eventually each task group came up with a one-day programme which was implemented on the Monday morning of the second week. During the week a video recording was made of each task group at work. During the second week, as part of a general evaluation of the success of the task group, this was played back to the group for analysis and discussion. Thus it was possible to examine the link between the group's effectiveness in working together and its end product.

Learning from this part of the course included the following:

1   Difficulties of forming a new working group and how to overcome them
2   Problems of making decisions and gaining commitment to them
3   How to obtain maximum benefit from everyone's ideas and previous training experience
4   Dealing with time pressures
5   Setting goals and targets
6   Finding specialist resources in the group and delegating tasks effectively

Group dynamics exercises

These were run for the members of the inexperienced T-group Monday to Thursday. The goal was to demonstrate the learning potential of several types of group dynamics exercises. They took place during the periods allocated to the three task groups so that members of those groups could, if they wished, observe and take part in the exercises. In this way all participants were able to broaden their experience of structured exercises.

By the end of the first week, participants were well grounded in the T-group method through personal experience and short lectures. They had also experienced a number of more structured situations, which also provided learning about group dynamics. The three task groups had produced plans for the secretarial trainees and had learned to distinguish work groups from T-groups, as two quite different situations requiring quite different intervention strategies from a trainer-consultant. This learning was to be deepened and reinforced by the events of the second week.

THE SECOND WEEK

T-groups

These continued from the first week, though at a frequency of one $1\frac{1}{2}$-hour session per day.

Task groups

All three one-day programmes designed in week one for secretarial trainees differed considerably. One emphasised career planning, another aimed to introduce them to what industry was like, and the third conducted several T-group exercises. The programmes were implemented on Monday. Tuesday was spent discussing the programmes and their effectiveness.

Free university

Ten and one-half hours were allotted in the second week to seminars and activities which were organised by either students or staff in order to meet more specialised learning needs of the students. The free university began with an inventory of course members' learning needs and the resources which they could offer to others. In the plenary room these needs and resources were collated and participants scheduled room and times for their activities, choosing which seminars they would attend at what times.

At any time, course members could make use of the video recordings which had been made of the inexperienced T-group. This led to discussing with the group's trainer his interventions and the effect of various members' contributions on the group. They were also able to see the stages by which this T-group developed.

Further seminars included:

1   Different types of group dynamics exercises about which people had knowledge
2   The design and evaluation of training courses
3   Group dynamics applications to industry
4   Approaches to organisation development
5   Diagnosis of group behaviour

The Polytechnic staff group

In order to demonstrate intervention into an on-going task group the Management Department staff volunteered to run a regular work meeting, consulted by its outside member. It was video-recorded for later analysis. The design for this session was as follows:

1   The staff group chose a current policy matter for discussion
2   The consultant sat somewhat outside the group near the video camera. He confined himself to helping the group clarify its task with interventions drawing attention to issues and problems which might be hindering effective group work
3   Course members were offered the chance to comment indirectly by writing proposed interventions on large pads, visible to the consultant, but not to the group consulted

This session turned out to be a highlight of the second week. A great deal of feeling was expressed and the meeting led to some sharp exchanges. It also went into points of unresolved conflicts of long standing, like the relative status and influence each member had in the group when it came to making a decision.

It will be understood that this staff group, responsible for the planning and running of the course, took a considerable risk in deciding to show its students their own group processes. On the one hand they risked that the meeting would become a battle, as it sometimes had done in the past; on the other hand, there was a likelihood that members would paper over their real problems and hide their feelings, particularly the interpersonal ones, in an effort to present an orderly front to their trainees. In the former situation they could justifiably be charged with not practising effective decision-making themselves while trying to show others how to do it; in the latter the projection of a safe facade would have reduced the learning opportunity for both themselves and the participants.

As it turned out the risk taken was justified. The interpersonal feelings, although uncomfortably acute at times were controlled and several useful decisions were reached in spite of the camera and arc lamps. The following are some of the comments made on the large sheets not visible at the time to the Polytechnic staff groups :

Why do they take so long to get started? They must be (a) used to each other, (b) full of ideas at this time.
What are the goals to which these issues relate?
I guess they need to listen to one another !
Too much effort to avoid leadership
If the group is not prepared to implement decisions and control the implementation, there is no point in planning as a group
Low-status members are committed to group decisions because it gives them equality of status

Talking afterwards about the experience of being observed in the situation, a member of the Polytechnic group said : 'It is very effective as a teaching experience : though most demanding for us. The difficulties of consulting a 'live' task group are dramatically illustrated.' Another said : 'It was really very hair raising to be in. I was initially worried but found it exhilirating once we got started. A great experiment! '

Personal counselling

The staff was available to counsel participants on their future development needs. For some this meant being invited back to the Polytechnic to co-train or to participate in future courses.

Closing session and exhibition of graffiti

A very informal closing session was planned in which participants could say anything they wanted about their experience during the two weeks.

Large sheets of newsprint papered the walls and many took the opportunity either to write or draw their views and feelings about the course. They described events and shared their experiences with those from other groups, milling about and rapidly turning the session into a party. The sayings of the great philosophers were thus inscribed on the wall.

CONCLUSION

There are few formal opportunities for trainers to develop techniques and skills, they must instead rely on their own experiences and those of their colleagues. The few courses which are aimed at developing trainer skills tend to spend very little time in working on application to one's back-home situation. With this in mind, a major goal of the organisers of the course for training trainers was to provide participants with practical situations within which they could learn and try out their training skills. Two experiences were specifically designed with this in mind. First, the trainees were provided with a 'real' course to plan and carry out. This involved considerable preparation, including a diagnosis of the training techniques available and detailed planning of how the course should be conducted. From this activity, trainees were able to practise and receive guidance on their skills and to consider with fellow participants the issues and problems involved in training. Second, an ongoing work group was observed in action and was analysed and counselled by the trainees. From this, the issues of dealing with and trying to help an ongoing task group were seen and later considered in length. At the time, these activities were extremely exciting and worthwhile and, according to follow-up questionnaires to participants, they led to considerable learning about training which could subsequently be used on the job. This emphasis on the unique aspects of the course should be viewed in perspective with the rest of the course which provided the core learning to the trainees. The T-group provided a basic experience in working in groups and helped to build a learning climate for the course.

The course design was developed to meet participant needs and goals as assessed both before the course and again at its mid-point.

Information about trainees' job situations and personal goals are essential to running any course but particularly when the course is aimed at application of teaching skills. As teachers and trainers it is extremely important to design a course from member goals, to innovate, and to re-think old ways of doing things. It was these things which led to excitement and learning for trainees and trainers alike.

Glossary

Action skills. Refers to the ability to act appropriately in a given situation, matching one's thoughts and feelings about what might be done to the behaviour of doing it. One of the main goals of group training is increasing one's range of behaviours so one may react flexibly to a greater number of situations. (Action skills = skills for action.)

Confrontation. Refers to opposing one particular set of beliefs, perceptions or behaviour patterns by a contrasting set — for example, between two people, two groups or a trainer and a group. It is through the recognition of these differences and subsequent experimentation with alternative beliefs or behaviour patterns that learning may occur. (This concept is elaborated in Harrison's model of T-group learning, see Chapter 9.)

Congruence. A concept initially developed by Carl Rogers, referring to the position where a person's feelings and behaviour are consistent. For example, the person who feels anger and expresses anger or who feels warmth and expresses warmth is being congruent. A congruent person is usually seen as authentic and genuine.

Cousins group. A training group composed of individuals of the same status level in an organisation who do not work closely together.

Coverdale training. A structured group-training approach developed by Coverdale, in which group members are given tasks to perform and on its completion evaluate their performance. From this they plan improvements for their next task and the cycle begins again.

<u>Diagnostic ability</u>.   Refers to the ability to assess accurately the dynamics of a situation. For example, heated disagreement may be diagnosed as a leadership struggle or as a simple disagreement; a silence in the group may be diagnosed as agreement to a decision or as reluctance to state disagreement. The diagnosis will depend on weighing up many factors in the situation such as the past history of the group, the needs of group members or the time of day. Increasing this ability to sense what is happening in a situation is a main goal of group training.

<u>Exercise</u>.   A structured situation or task with given rules and objectives. Its purpose is to generate behaviour in a relevant area. This behaviour can subsequently be discussed and conclusions drawn from the information (or data) that has emerged. For example the group may be given a particular task which will highlight the effectiveness of problem solving and communication skills; a task which may be real life or imaginary and in which people may be asked to play roles or be themselves. It is in the discussion and conclusions that learning often emerges.

<u>Family group</u>.   A training group composed of individuals who work together on a day-to-day basis. A training programme for family groups is generally more structured than for either stranger or cousin groups and focuses on work problems and work relationships.

<u>Feedback</u>.   Telling a person or a group the impression he or they make or the effect he or they may have on another is called giving feedback. For example : 'I feel pressured by you to do what you want to do,' or 'When you ask my opinion I find it is easier to work cooperatively with you.' This sort of behaviour is often encouraged in group training in order to diagnose a group situation or to help the person or group gain an increased awareness of how he or they are seen and how his or their behaviour affects others.

<u>Group dynamics</u>.   A field of study concerned with knowledge about the nature of groups, the patterns of their development and their interrelationships with individuals, other groups and larger institutions. Examples of specific areas of study are : communication processes, the effect of leadership styles on group decision-making and factors influencing group solidarity and productiveness.

<u>Group dynamics training</u>.   Refers to any training that is aimed at increasing people's understanding of the nature of groups and the processes underlying group behaviour such as leadership, decision-making and motivation. It may be studied in a variety of ways from group training to role playing, case studies or lectures.

<u>Group process</u>.   A series of conscious or unconscious actions or occurrences underlying the tangible content of what is going on in a group.

The dynamics of a group at work can be considered from two levels : the content or subject matter of what is said and done and the process of how it is said and done. For example, the content may be a discussion of the Common Market or building a bridge whereas the process may be an open discussion, an argument, or a lengthy statement by the chairman; it may be high involvement or boredom; it may be a strategic jockeying for position or an open sharing of information. The group process affects the productiveness of the group, how people feel about decisions, and people's commitment to the implementation of decisions. In group training, con- siderable time is taken up with trying to understand the group process and its relationship to task effectiveness.

Group training. Refers to a variety of approaches to training which involves learning from one's own experience by evaluating the group's or individual's performance and by experimentation with new behaviours or methods of working in the group. It is a type of group dynamics training. The specific group-training approach may be highly structured, such as Grid or Coverdale Training, or may be relatively unstructured, such as T-group training.

Here and now. Refers to the focusing on the immediate group or personal situation (here) and the present point in time (now). This is different from focusing on past events or possible future occurrences. Concentrating on the 'here and now' provides data on the group or interpersonal processes and enables discussion to take place on how people feel about the group situation or one another.

Identification. A process of influence, defined by Kelman, where an individual accepts the influence of another because he sees the other as an ideal figure. For example, a course member may see the group trainer as an ideal person and therefore try to imitate him and behave as he thinks the trainer would behave. (Further discussion of the value of identification as an influence process in behavioural change can be found in Chapter 1 and Chapter 10.)

In-company course. A course whose membership is restricted to a single firm and which is usually designed specifically to meet the needs of that firm. If it is an in-company course it is likely to focus more on work relationships and problems of work groups with specific tasks and less on personal relationships than a stranger group. There are several varieties of composition depending on the training goals :

Individuals of the same status level (horizontal slice or cousins group)
Individuals of different status level who do not work closely with one another (diagonal slice)
Individuals who work together, typically a boss and his subordinates (vertical slice or family group)

177

Internalisation.   A process of influence, defined by Kelman, where an individual accepts influence in order to maintain his actions and beliefs consistent with his values. (Further discussion of the value of internal-isation as an influence process in behaviour change can be found in Chapter 1 and Chapter 10.)

Laboratory training.   A name sometimes given to the T-group although it really refers to any course where the emphasis is on a laboratory approach to learning. A laboratory approach is one that encourages:

1   The collection of data, for example about how different group members perceive events and one another
2   Experimentation with different styles of interpersonal behaviour and group work
3   The evaluation by group members of events and group effectiveness

Management development.   A general term for any planned activity con-cerned with increasing individual managerial effectiveness either through improving skills, increasing knowledge or by changing attitudes. It may involve such things as job rotation, performance appraisals, objective setting, training or career planning. Whilst its emphasis is on the individual manager, as opposed to the group, department or organisation, it may well be seen as a contribution to an overall organisation develop-ment programme.

Managerial Grid training.   A six-phase group-training approach of a structured nature developed by Blake and Mouton. The phases are concerned with: educating the manager about the grid approach and about basic leadership skills, team building, intergroup relations, business strategy and diagnosing organisational problems.

Open course: See stranger group

Organisation development (OD).   Concerned with increasing the ability of the organisation to meet the environmental problems that it may face. It tends to be a total approach to the organisation, is frequently of a planned development nature and concentrates primarily on groups within the organisation. Organisation development activities tend to be long term, focused on action and on changing attitudes and behaviour. Generally they consist of some form of group training, target and goal setting or inter-group relations training. Needs for organisation development often occur when an organisation is concerned with managing change and with improving the performance and value of its human resources.

Process consultancy.   Consultant activities which aim to help a family group or organisation unit to improve its process of working together. An example would be a consultant sitting in on a group meeting and helping the group to focus on communication difficulties or decision-making procedures. (See group process.)

Role.   A pattern of actions or behavioural requirements associated with a job position which the occupant is expected to perform. For a manager, for example, this may include : leading subordinates, dressing in a suit, working certain hours, behaving in a certain manner to his superiors, and achieving certain performance standards. The role may vary according to various factors such as the specific company, status level and function of the person concerned.

Sensitivity.   Refers to the ability to sense reactions and feelings in an interpersonal situation. Improving an individual's sensitivity is one of the main goals of group training.

Sensitivity training.   Another name for T-group training.

Stranger group.   A course whose membership is open to individuals from various organisations. On this sort of course, participants generally do not know one another. This minimises the long-term consequences of what occurs during the group and tends to reduce the individual's risk of getting involved and being open, thus facilitating the establishment of a learning climate.

Structure.   A framework, set of ground rules, or formal roles and procedures within which people are required to work. A structured training session is one in which certain overt roles, procedures or objectives are provided by the trainer. Absence of overt structure from the trainer does not however mean that no structure will be present, for people require varying degrees of structure for their activities and will seek covertly or overtly to provide this. Focusing on changes in structure and people's feelings about this is often an aim of group training.

Study group.   A term used in connection with the Leicester, Tavistock and Grubb Institute group-training courses. It is similar to a T-group except that the trainer's role places greater emphasis on the diagnosis of group process and less emphasis on expressing his own feelings and making direct suggestions.

Reddin three-dimensional grid.   A structured group-training approach developed by Reddin which places considerable emphasis on the development of a range of leadership styles.

T-group training.   A type of group training in which participants learn by studying the group of which they are a part : why it is the way it is and the effects of group members on one another. If differs from other group-training approaches in that there is a minimum amount of structure provided by the training staff. The goals are to increase members' sensitivity and the ability to diagnose or analyse group behaviour and to increase members' effectiveness in action skills appropriate to a given situation.

T-group seminar.   See T-group training

Team training or team building.   See family group

Trainer.   'A tall bronzed person with leopardskin trunks who jumps through hoops, runs around in circles and holds everyone else's tail in his trunk.'
     Staff member with responsibility for running a group, there may be one or two trainers per group. Although the trainer may not actively lead the group, he nevertheless exerts considerable influence on group members by what he does and does not do. His goal is to facilitate the meeting of group goals. To do this he may diagnose group events, express his own feelings, provide support to individuals and the group, as well as encouraging group members to do the same. The trainer may also plan and introduce exercises in order to help the group. Trainer development involves several experiences of being in groups as a participant and further experience as a co-trainer with a more experienced trainer.

Unstructured group.   One feature of most T-groups is their relatively unstructured nature. Though not devoid of any structure, such things as procedures for decision-making, setting an agenda or topic for discussion, and prescribed roles such as group leader, chairman, or scribe are not formally imposed by the staff. Rather, each group must develop its own structure which it may subsequently modify in order to improve the group's effectiveness or to experiment with different styles of group work. (See structure.)

Some training centres

Action Training: The Industrial Society, Robert Hyde House, 48 Bryanston Square, London W1H 8AH.

Bath University, School of Management, Rockwell, Kings Weston Road, Bristol, BS11 0UY.

Coverdale Training: 57 Denison House, 296 Vauxhall Bridge Road, London SW1.

ERGOM: Predikherenberg 55, 3200 Kessel-16, Belgium.

European Institute for Trans-National Studies in Group and Organisational Development (EIT) Secretary General: Trygve Johnstad, Box 104, 1364 Hvalstad, Norway.

Group Relations Training Association: c/o Ken Harrison, 7 Grange Park Avenue, Wilmslow, Cheshire.

Grubb Institute of Behavioural Studies: 1 Whitehall Place, London SW1.

Gunnar Hjelholt Ass. Valkendorfsgade 19, 1151 Copenhagen K, Denmark.

National Training Laboratories, 1201 Sixteenth Street, N W Washington DC, USA.

NIPG/TNO, Wassenarserweg 56, Leiden, Holland.

Managerial Grid : Scientific Methods, Inc, Box 195, Austin, Texas, 78767, USA.

North London Polytechnic, Applied Behavioural Science Division, 129-131 Camden High Street, London NW1.

Tavistock Institute of Human Relations, 120 Belsize Lane, London NW3.

Team-Co, Frederiksborggade 9, 1360, Copenhagen K, Denmark.

TSR (Nederlandse Vereniging van Trainers in Sociale Relaties volgens de laboratorium methode) Bottisellistraat 8, Amsterdam, Holland.

University of Dublin, Department of Business Studies, Trinity College, Dublin 2, Ireland.

University of Leeds, Department of Management Studies, Leeds 2, Yorkshire.

Further reading

Beckhard, R, Organization Development : Strategies and Models
  (Reading Mass., Addison-Wesley, 1969).
Bennis, W G, Organization Development : Its Nature, Origins and
  Prospects (Reading Mass., Addison-Wesley, 1969).
Blake, R R & Mouton, J S The Managerial Grid (Houston, Gulf
  Publishing, 1964).
Blake, R R & Mouton, J S Building a Dynamic Corporation through Grid
  Organization Development (Reading, Mass., Addison-Wesley, 1969).
Bradford, L P, Gibb, J R & Benne, K D (eds) T-group Theory and
  Laboratory Method : Innovation in Re-education (New York, Wiley,
  1964).
Cooper, C L 'An evaluation of sensitivity training', Industrial Training
  International, 1967.
Cooper, C L & Mangham, I L (eds) T-groups : A Survey of Research
  (New York, Wiley, 1971).
Emery, F E (ed) Systems Thinking (Harmondsworth, Penguin, 1969).
Golembiewski, R T & Blumberg (eds) Sensitivity Training and the Lab
  Approach : Readings about Concepts and Applications (Itasca, Ill.,
  F E Peacock Publishers Inc., 1970).
Gosling, R, Miller, R H, Woodhouse, D & Turguet, P M The Use of
  Small Groups in Training (New York, Grune & Stratton, 1967).
Harrison, R, 'Choosing the depth of organization intervention', Journal
  of Applied Behavioural Science, 6 (1970), 181-202.
Lawrence, P R & Lorsch, J W Developing Organizations : Diagnosis and
  Action (Reading, Mass., Addison-Wesley, 1969).

Miles, M B 'Changes during and following laboratory training',
    Journal of Applied Behavioural Science, 1 (1965), 215-42.
Pfeiffer, J W & Jones, J E, A Handbook of Structured Exercises for
    Human Relations Training (Iowa, University Associates Press, 1969).
Rice, A K, Learning for Leadership (London, Tavistock Publications,
    1965).
Schein, E H, Process Consultation : Its Role in Organization Development
    (Reading, Mass., Addison-Wesley, 1969).
Schein, E H & Bennis, W G Personal and Organization Change through
    Group Methods : The Laboratory Approach (New York, Wiley, 1965).
Smith, P B, Improving Skills in Working with People : the T-group
    (London, HMSO, 1969).
Smith, P B & Honour, T F, 'The impact of phase I Managerial Grid
    training', Journal of Management Studies, 6 (1969).
Walton, R E Interpersonal Peacemaking : Confrontations and Third
    Party Consultation (Reading, Mass., Addison-Wesley, 1969).
Whitaker, G (ed) T-group Training : Group Dynamics in Management
    Education (Oxford, Basil Blackwell, 1965).

Index

Action skills 137, 138
Action training 5, 101 et seq
Adair, John : three overlapping circles 108
Application of learning 153, 154
Appointed leader, role of 39
Argument : listening to opponent 76
Argyle, Michael 29
Argyris, C 71, 163, 164
Attitude change ('unfreezing and
   refreezing') 127-129
Attitude of course members 46
Autocratic style 151

Barrett-Lennard, G T 162
Batchelder, R L and Hardy, J M 30
Bath/Tavistock laboratories 101
Beckhard, R 84, 149
Behaviour analysis 122 et seq
Behaviour change 122, 124
Berger, M L 122, 151
Bion, W R 31
Blake, R R and Mouton's Managerial
   Grid 31, 49 et seq
Blake, R R : 'T-group theory and the
   laboratory method' 159

Bolman, L G 160, 162, 164
Breakdown, mental 149, 154
Bridger, H 36
Bunker, D R 152, 153;
    personal change categories 139
    system of behaviour
      categories 122, 123
Burt, H E 128
Business games 45

Campbell, J P 159
Campbell, J P and Dunnette, M
  29, 69
Cardboard squares exercise 77
Case studies 45
Centres of group training for
 industry 30
Christie, R 153
Commitment 9
Conflict, avoidance of 76
    free association with 76
Confrontation and support 28
Confrontation meeting 84
·Congruence-empathy by trainer 162
Consultancy, demand for 95
Consultant's role, presentation of
  111, 113
Consulting relationship 112
Contract setting 87, 116
    and quid pro quo 87, 88
Cooper, C L 122, 159, 163, 164
Cousin group, definition 2
    reaction 3
Coverdale 83
    training 31, 32
Crozier, Michael 37
Crying 30
Culbert, S A 161, 162, 164
Cultural island 27, 28

Demarcation 55
Democratic style 151
Deutsch, M 160
Diagnostic skill 137, 138
Direction by trainer, degree of 28
Dunnette, M D 159

EIT organisation laboratories 101
Emery, F E and Trist, E 37
Emotional arousal 149
Encounter groups 2
Escalation of conflict 93
European Institute for Transnational
  Studies in Group and Organisational
  Development (EIT) 31
Evaluation of internal courses 46
Evaluation 10
    questionnaire 60
Experimental learning 1
External consultants 10
    courses 10

Family group, definition 2
    reaction 3
Feedback 16, 17, 19, 25
Fleishman, E A 128, 144
Follow-up 93
Force field analysis 107
Ford Motor Credit Co 7, 134 et seq
Foremen's attitude 128
Fraser, J M 147
Free university 172
Friedlander, F 69

Gil, P and Bennis, W G 136
Goals of T-group training 15, 16, 27
Graffiti 173, 174
Grid training 4, 31
Group dynamics exercises 171
Group Relations Training
  Association 31
Grubb Institute of Behavioural
  Science 31
Grubb/Tavistock 'organisation and
  authority' laboratories 100
Guardedness and inhibition 20, 21

Handy, Charles, director of Sloan
  School of Management Studies 37
Hardert, R 151, 160
Harris, E F 128
Harrison, Roger 73, 114, 150, 155, 160
    four-step selection 150
'Human Nature and Organisational
  Reality' - Chris Argyris film 109

IBM (UK) Ltd 5, 98 et seq
ICI Pharmaceuticals and grid
  training 4, 55 et seq
Incentive schemes 55
Incompetence 22, 26
Industrial Society : 'Action Centred
  Leadership' courses 100
Industrial Training Boards 34
Internal course, design of 44
Internalisation 29
Interim evaluation 46
Intimidation 24, 25
Invisible management college 42
Issue diagnosis 89

Kelman, H C 29
    theory of social influence 162

Learning to learn 42
Leeds University 30
    consultancy skills laboratory 101
    department of management 151
Lewin's stages of personal change
  125, 127
Likert, R 80
  ·diagnostic instrument 56
Lohmann, K 160
Lubin, B 149, 150

Management by objectives
  (MBO) 5, 69-71, 79
Management style and
  participation 152
Managerial Grid , guidelines
  for use of 64, 65
'Managerial Grid', the book,
  criticism of 58
Manager's role 4
Mangham, I L 159
Mangham, I L and Cooper, C L
  29, 69
Mann, R D 160
Marital conflict 86
Massarik, R 159
Mathis, A G 128
McGregor's classification of
  management style 137

McGregor's theories 56
Method of T-group training 16, 17
Miles, M B 144, 147, 151
Moscow, D 123, 144

National Training Laboratories 30
Negotiation of issues 92
North London Polytechnic 30
North London Polytechnic
  management department 168 et seq

Open-system organisation 37
Organisational climate 141, 142
Organisational self-review 35
Organisation development (OD),
  definition 2
Organisation laboratory 104 et seq
    course programme 106
Osgood's semantic differential
  scale 123
Owen, Robert 81

Participative behaviours 151, 152
Pepitone, A 160
Perceived effectiveness 29
Personal change 139, 161
    self 140
    as seen by others 140
Personal counselling 173
Personality clash 115
Peters, D R 160, 161, 163
Planning of training 9
Power and influence problems
  84, 85
Problem analysis 136, 137
Problem census 142
Process consultancy 5
Programme in Organisation
  Development 101
Psathas, G 151, 160
Psychological damage 30

Quid pro quo 87, 88
    example of 93

Reddin 71
Reisel, J 160

Resistance to programme 10
Rice, A K 31
Rogers, C R 162
Role definition 85
Role negotiation 5, 85 et seq
   and trust 86
   dynamics of 94, 95
   economics of 95
   summary 96, 97
   when and where 87

Satisfaction and dissatisfaction
 at work 78
Schein, E H and Bennis, W G
 127, 128, 130, 164
Schein's decision making
 methods 107
Scientific Methods Inc (SMI) 57
Selection 10
   for training 148 et seq, 154, 155
Self-appraisal 47
Self-change 140
Self-disclosure by trainer 161
Sensitivity training 83
   problems of 69
'Sick' - definition 149
SLICE (sensitivity, listening,
 interviewing, counselling, empathy)
 102, 103
Smith, P B 155, 164
Smith, P B and Honour, T F 31
Social influence 162
Status mix 59
Stermerding, A H 160
Stock, D 128
Stranger group, definition 2
   reaction 3
Suggestion schemes 55
Suitability for training 148 et seq,
 154, 155
Support and confrontation 28, 73
Sykes, A J M 128

Tannenbaum, R 159
Task groups 170
Tavistock Institute of Human
 Relations, London 31

Team building 5
    consultancy 111 et seq
Teamwork questionnaire 72, 73
    discrepancies 76
'Tell and sell' teaching
 methods 167
Theory X and Theory Y
 (McGregor) 137 et seq
T-group origins 2
T-groups at IBM 99
Threats, legitimate use of, and
 limitations of 88
Top management, role of 40
Trainer, assessment of 159 et seq
Trainer's role 7
Trainer training 167 et seq
Tregoe, Kepner 83

Unlearning and relearning 38

Vansina, L 160
Video recordings 172
Video tape recorder 169
    use of in training 171
Visitors' role in courses 109
Vulnerability 25

Weekly staff agreement (WSA) 57
Weschler, I R 159, 160
Work climate 123
Work relationships 6
Written suggestions, uneasiness
 over 94, 95

YMCA, American 30

Zander, A 160
Zenger, J H 160
Zuckerman, M 149